The Factor of Eighteen

John Blankenship

Avid Readers Publishing Group
Lakewood, California

The opinions expressed in this manuscript are those of the author and do not represent the thoughts or opinions of the publisher. The author warrants and represents that he has the legal right to publish or owns all material in this book. If you find a discrepancy, contact the publisher at www.avidreaderspg.com.

The Factor of Eighteen

Avid Readers Publishing Group

http://www.avidreaderspg.com

ISBN-13: 978-1-61286-173-9

Printed in the United States

Table of Contents

Introduction v

Chapter 1 – Creating a Masterpiece 1

Chapter 2 - Start With the End in Mind 3

Chapter 3 - Lessons Learned 9

Chapter 4 - Stumbling Blocks 30

Chapter 5 - Key Ingredients 62

Chapter 6 – A Message for the Youth 79

Chapter 7 - Testimonies 88

Conclusion 108

Introduction

The title of this book stems from a conversation I had with a good friend of mine, Dr. Dwaine Cales, father of four children. I taught two of his kids and know them well. All four have turned out to be extremely talented, successful, and productive adults.

Dwaine has the ability to invest in and add value to his children and other people. He has a great relationship with all of his kids. They love and respect him greatly.

When my wife and I had our son, I knew exactly whom to seek for parenting advice. The nugget of information that stood out to me was when Dwaine asked me, "What kind of a person do you want your son to be when he is eighteen? Determine that early and raise him accordingly." How I raise my son must funnel him in that direction. I must model those desired traits in my own life. That does not mean I determine how he is going to live his life. It does not mean I will make decisions for him. However, it provides a framework for me as I try to be the best father I can be. *The Factor of Eighteen* basically says to start with the end in mind.

My son is now five. I'm in no hurry for him to be eighteen, but I am anxious to see what type of young man he becomes. What I don't want to do is wake up one morning and realize I had no game plan to help mold my son into the type of person God wants him to be. This book will flesh out some of the ideas that I have learned and observed through fifteen years of teaching and coaching. I hope you will find this book to be very practical and useful as you search for ways to improve your relationship with your children. The book is designed to be a very casual and quick read. My intentions are that you can begin implementing these ideas within one to three days. Your children are certainly worth the investment.

Chapter 1
Creating a Masterpiece

Proverbs 22:6 - "Train up a child in the way he should go and when he is old he will not depart from it."

Parenting is both fun and challenging. We all love our kids. We all want them to be successful and live productive lives. However, it doesn't always work that way. Ask any parent who has a child in jail, using drugs, or living on the streets. That was never part of the plan. In his book, *Parenting Principles From the Heart of a Pediatrician*, Dr. William Slonecker says, "What are we trying to accomplish with parenting? We must begin not with the tools, not even with the canvas, but with the finished masterpiece hung perfectly on our favorite wall, framed in all its splendor and grandeur." I think he is saying we should begin with the end in mind. Have you thought through what you want your child to be like when he/she is eighteen? I don't mean their physical appearance, but their character, attitude, level of integrity, their faith etc…

A builder knows what the house is going to look like before he ever begins building it. The plans are finalized before he raises a hammer. No boards are cut until the measurements have been checked twice. Parenting should be no different. We should have a finished product in mind. We will make mistakes along the way, but do we know what we are trying to accomplish as we raise our children? Obviously, there are variables in parenting. Some of those might be out of our control. However, we can make sure our child-rearing procedures align with our values. We can make sure we are moving our children in the direction we want them to progress. As a Christian parent, I want to teach my son how to hunger and thirst for righteousness; that would be part of the end product. We as parents have to model that for them. Josh Billings said, "Train up a child in the way he should go - and walk there yourself once in a while."

Chapter 1 thought questions:

1. What goals do you have for your children?

2. Would improving your relationship with your children help them reach those goals? Why or why not?

3. In terms of how your children turn out, what will your masterpiece look like?

Chapter 2
Start With the End in Mind

The birth of my son radically changed my life. Things will never be the same. One small example - what I watch on television has changed. I've traded Fox News for Curious George. Watching sports has been replaced by Martha Speaks. Word World has overtaken the evening news. I've missed a couple of exciting overtime basketball games so my son could watch Barney. Before I had a child, I didn't like Barney. Now that I have a child and **have** to watch Barney, I'm ready to slap the purple off of him. Naps, relaxing, and setting my own schedule, well, those have changed too. As a parent, can you relate? It doesn't matter though, does it? My love for him and my desire to be with him supersedes my agenda. Your children's future well-being may depend on these influential moments you make for them now. Are you a key influence in their lives? Are you making time to cultivate a deeper relationship with them? If you don't, others will. They **will** be influenced by someone. It should be you, the parent. What I say and how I conduct myself matters. My son is watching what I do. I'm glad he's observing me because I have total control over my conduct. I can do my best to model those traits I hope he develops in his life.

This is why my relationship with him is so important. I don't want him turning to the wrong people for guidance. He loves me and enjoys being with me at the age of five. How long will that continue? Will the structure of our relationship change? I pray it won't, because I want him to trust and love me as much when he is eighteen as he does now. What can parents do to build stronger and lasting relationships with their kids? That question deserves careful consideration.

What is your greatest priority in life? Maybe it's your faith, spouse, or your job. If you have children, hopefully they rank close to the top. I have worked with twelve to eighteen year olds since 1997. I've seen healthy and unhealthy relationships between parents and their kids. What's the difference? Why does one family thrive while another struggles to co-exist? Why do some kids want to spend time with their parents and others are eager to leave? We have to ask ourselves what we are trying to accomplish with our kids. What is the end result when it comes to raising our children?

As a teacher, when I prepare lessons for class, I have objectives for each lesson. These are the things I want my students to learn from that particular lesson. I design my lessons around those objectives and determine the best teaching method to accomplish those desired results. I also coach basketball. Coaching is no different. For a few practices we might focus on our defensive rotation out of a trap, or we might work on our press breakers. Whatever it might be, I have a plan. I know what the end result should look like. It's just a matter of choosing the right concepts and drills to accomplish those objectives. In fact, I usually have an overall scope of the entire season in mind as I plan out practices. By the end of the season, this is what I want my team to know. It's my master plan. Because of this I never walk into practice thinking, what should we work on today? It's planned to the last minute. My players would attest to this fact. I have very precise practice plans with each drill beginning and ending at a certain time. For fun, during one of our team bonding parties, some of my players made a schedule for the activities that looked something like this:

1. 5:00 – 5:28 – Eat pizza
2. 5:28 – 6:03 - Play games
3. 6:03 – 8:03 – Watch movie
4. 8:03 – 9:10 – Goal setting

It might be one of those things you had to be there to appreciate, but we all got a good laugh from it. I appreciated their sarcasm. I told them I wanted to prove I could be flexible and stray from my original practice plans. To prove it, I lengthened the time allotted for sprints at our next practice. You adjust when needed, but this gives you a plan to maximize your time and achieve the desired results. I take my job as a coach very seriously. I want to prepare my athletes so we can win. However, at the end of the day, it's still just a game. If I am willing to begin with the end in mind for basketball, it seems crazy to me not to do the same for my child.

As I type this, there are about two weeks left in the school year. In a few short months another school year will be here. For many parents it will be different this time. Your children will not be coming home each night. They are leaving for college. Picture this scenario with me.

It's the middle of August and I'm certain there are tears being shed. Parents are embracing their sons and daughters one last time before they drive to college for the first time. As they embrace, there are eighteen years of memories scrolling through the parent's minds. The drive home from the hospital, the first birthday, playing catch in the back yard, family vacations, daughters cooking with moms, sons helping their dads in the shop, and the list of wonderful memories continue to flood the mind.

But now, in that moment of embrace, you realize your child is transitioning to a different phase of life. You cling to those memories while praying you have instilled proper values. They are leaving. They aren't going to the store. They aren't visiting grandma for the day. They are headed to one of the most pivotal moments of their lives. Persuasive professors, irreligious roommates, peer pressured parties and a host of other stumbling blocks will be awaiting their arrival.

Your three year old who used to jump into your arms will now be considering new ideas and philosophies different from the foundational values you taught. You can only hope and pray they remain faithful to what you have taught them.

As your child drives away to college, what are you thinking? I'm guessing at that moment modeling integrity and spending time with your child seems far more important than the extra hour at the office or watching another football game on television. I have several more years before I have to deal with this. However, this is a great reminder of what is really important. I must begin with the end in mind. I must make it a priority to instill godly values in my son.

I encourage parents with younger children to fast forward to that final embrace and determine right now what will be important to you at that moment. You should model integrity, love your kids, and value them. If you do those things, they will learn to trust you early and will continue to do so at those pivotal moments later in life. Take some serious time and determine what path you want your children to choose. Pray about it; discuss it with your spouse and do it soon.

If you do not have children, you obviously have plenty of time to think through this. If you have children, it's not too late. Just know it becomes more difficult the longer you wait. If you have not invested in your child to this point, they may be a little resistant at first. This may require some patience on your part. May God give you wisdom and direction as you invest in your greatest joy – your children.

Chapter 2 thought questions:

1. What does it mean to you to start with the end in mind?
2. What does that mean in terms of raising your kids?
3. Will thinking about how you want them to be when they are eighteen impact how you raise them today? If so, how? If not, why not?

4. Are there unnecessary things or events in your life that might be stealing away needed time with your children? If so, what are they and what will you do about it?

Chapter 3
Lessons Learned

In this chapter I want to share some key lessons I have learned from personal experiences with my own son, and situations I have observed between my students, athletes, and their parents. These lessons are not intended to be a systematic approach in how I share them, but rather a wide scope of experiences that will hopefully resonate with people experiencing different phases of life with their children.

Must Be Present To Win

Don't you hate those, "have to be present to win," moments? The good prizes are always given at the end. It's intentional to keep you there as long as possible. It's part of their devious plan. You get tired, you get bored, you get frustrated, and so you go home. Obviously, if you stay, your name will never be chosen for the grand prize. If your luck is like mine, you will never win anyway. It seems logical to leave and go home early. However, if you leave, then your name will be called for sure. It's a lose lose situation. I have seen people miss out on a new car, an Ipad, and a GPS system because they didn't want to remain until the very end of the drawings. I'm sure there were some deep regrets, especially from the person who lost the car.

It's no different in the lives of our children. The stakes are just a lot higher. You have to be present in their lives to win. As I mentioned earlier, someone will influence your kids. Who is it going to be? Assuming you are being a positive influence, you and your kids both win if you are involved in their lives. Sometimes kids, especially as they get older, will pretend they don't care whether you are there or not. My observations have demonstrated the opposite.

Most of my basketball players really appreciate it when their parents attend their games, especially when they are supportive. Knowing their parents love them and care enough to be there is important to them. I very seldom see this appreciation communicated to their parents. However, I know it's true because I have seen their reactions when their parents are not at their games. They want you in their lives. They need you in their lives. You must be present to win with them.

When my son was four, he reminded me of the importance of being there. I woke up early one morning and couldn't get back to sleep. I prayed and asked God to teach me something that day. I didn't expect it to happen within minutes.

It stormed all night so I decided to sleep on a mattress next to my son's bed. (He is not a big fan of thunderstorms.) The next morning, at 5:15, I heard my son squirming in bed. I looked up and saw him leaning over his bed railing. He spoke these precious words, "I love you daddy." It was a tender, sweet moment, even at 5:15 in the morning. I told him I loved him as well. That was enough. He went back to sleep, or so I thought. Approximately fifteen minutes later he came and joined me on the mattress. Thinking I was asleep prompted these words from him. "Daddy, I'm sorry I woke you but I wanted to be close to you."

It was in that very moment, that fraction of a second, that God reminded me of this simple truth. He just wants to spend time with us. Amazing! The Creator wants to be close to His creation. We shouldn't expect it to be different with human relationships. Parents, we have to be present in their lives to win with them. We cannot develop influence from a distance.

When my son joined me on the twin mattress, I lost any free space. He stole most of the blanket. He bumped my head with his. He flopped around like a fish out of water. My comfort went to discomfort. Calm went to chaos. Rest went to restlessness and yet I was beyond contentment as my son settled into my arms and chest. It was a wonderful few minutes before being interrupted by his desire to watch cartoons and my need to get ready for work.

Look for those sweet moments of intimacy with your child. The level of intimacy changes with age, of course. But don't miss those moments in the chaos of life. Don't forget those moments with God. He desires them too.

Lessons Learned – Fishing With a Four Year Old

Fishing is always a fun adventure with a four year old. We had a great time and I can't wait to do it again soon. I noticed a few similarities between fishing and parenting that I want to share.

1. **Fishing and parenting both require patience.** Fortunately, the fish were active that night. My son didn't have to wait very long between catches. The few times he did have to wait, he would drop his fishing pole and find something else to do. When he got his fishing line hung up on something, he didn't want to wait for me to fix it. His lack of patience required more patience from me. If I was going to use this as a bonding and teaching night with my son, patience was necessary. Many things can zap our patience. Lack of sleep, a bad day at work, struggles at home, etc… What do we teach our kids in these moments of anger and frustration? Patience is not the absence of discipline and accountability. However, do we as parents ever get angry at our kids when it should be directed at something else? It's easy to transfer it to them. I can't think of a faster way to hinder relational growth with our kids.

What is the typical result when you lose patience with your child? How does that impact your relationship with him or her? Remember the factor of eighteen. What values are you trying to instill in them by the time they are eighteen? The

Bible has much to say about anger. Here are a few examples from the New International Version.

Proverbs15:1 – "A gentle answer turns away wrath, but a harsh word stirs up anger."

Proverbs 29:11- "A fool gives full vent to his anger, but a wise man keeps himself under control."

James 1:19 & 20 – "My dear brothers, take note of this: Everyone should be quick to listen, slow to speak and slow to become angry, for man's anger does not bring about the righteous life that God desires."

Discipline is necessary, beneficial, and even biblical. However, discipline should be prompted by love and not anger. Anger may prompt the discipline, but love better guide how it is implemented. Would an added dose of patience be just what is needed to use those moments for relational growth between you and your child? Please do not misunderstand my point. Parents need to discipline their children as often as necessary, but there are times we miss opportunities to teach because our anger dictates our response. It takes far more energy to teach our children when we are frustrated than it does to discipline them when we are angry.

I have been fishing enough to know when you get impatient you lose opportunities to catch fish. You reel your line in too soon or too fast and miss the opportunity to catch something good. The same is true with our children. We miss teachable moments when we lose our patience. Practice patience; it will make you a better fisherman and parent.

2. **Stay focused.** My son and I originally thought we would keep a few of the fish we caught. So, after catching them, we placed them on a stringer and put them back in the water. Every five minutes or so, Marcus (my son), sat his pole down and ran over to look at the fish we caught. Several times he missed an opportunity to catch another fish because he was not focused in the moment.

How many times do we plan to spend quality time with our kids only to have it interrupted by less important things? We answer phone calls, watch television, or work on job related things. I'm quite certain we could increase our relational growth with our children if we stayed focused on spending time with them. I met a friend at Chick-fil-A for lunch one afternoon. Sitting at the table next to us was a father and son. The boy looked about seven or eight. I wasn't eavesdropping, but they were talking loud enough that I could hear their conversation. I could tell by their discussion this was a planned outing on their part. The boy was excited to eat lunch with his dad. I was excited for him. Then, the boy's smile immediately left his face when he heard his dad's phone ring. I saw the dad reach for his phone. I assumed he was going to turn it off so he could enjoy lunch with his son.

For the next twenty minutes the dad talked on the phone while his son sat there basically eating lunch alone. This moment was big in the eyes of the boy. The dad had a chance to show value to his son and spend quality time with him. He chose to lose his focus. He lost the reason why he was there in the first place. The conversation on the phone was casual. It was not an important call he had to take. He blew that moment with his son. Remember the factor of eighteen. What we do each day with our children impacts the final result. It's important to keep your focus.

3. <u>The deeper we went the bigger the fish</u> - This was certainly true on that night. We fished in the shallow waters at first and caught a couple of perch. Later we went to deeper waters and caught much bigger fish. He had more fun catching the bigger ones. It required more effort to get them to shore, but the battle was worth it. You know where I'm headed, right? It's easy to spend shallow moments with our kids. It takes much more effort and time to develop deeper, more meaningful relationships with them. Remember, your kids will be influenced by someone. Let it be you. Spend deep moments with your kids. The results will be worth it.

The key is showing value to what they value. You might enjoy doing a particular thing, but if your child does not enjoy that, it will be a shallow moment to them. Listen to your child. Know what they enjoy doing. What are their interests? Plan to spend time doing activities that your children enjoy.

When they sense you care about them and what they truly care about, it will break down barriers that will allow for deeper moments with your kids. You will get a great return on your investment. It builds trust with them. It allows you to have influence with them. It puts you in a position to develop those key characteristics you want them to possess when they are eighteen.

Remember these key lessons that apply both to fishing and parenting: They require patience. They require you to stay focused. The deeper you go, the better the results will be.

Lessons Learned – Observations

The Factor of Eighteen is all about what you can do between now and your child's eighteenth birthday to make them the kind of person you want, they want, and most importantly God wants them to be. In this section of the chapter I want to share a few of the observations I have made as a teacher. Some of these I've experienced with my own son as well. Experience really can be a good teacher. To some extent, parenting skills can be developed through trial and error. That's why it makes sense to learn from others. Find parents who have great relationships with their kids and invite them to lunch. Ask them questions. Seek their advice and take detailed notes. You can also read parenting books, watch DVD's and attend parenting classes or seminars. Professional development is a big concept in the business world. We even hear it often as teachers. All of us should be learning and becoming better at what we do. Why shouldn't that carry over to parenting? Everyone could learn something that would help them become a better parent. Allow me to share a few of these observations that I believe can make us better parents.

1. Pursue Their Passions – One important lesson I learned prior to having my own child is this. Parents that have great relationships with their children make it a priority to invest in an area in which their children have a passion. I'm not implying you always make your children the center of attention. However, you do need to understand what is important to them and what motivates them. Determine what they value and spend time doing those things with them. That allows you to pursue their passions and that gives you influence. Influence is incredibly important in the factor of eighteen. Once you know their passions, you can use them as a vehicle to cultivate deeper relationships with your kids.

My son loves to watch backhoes and dump trucks. We will occasionally drive around looking for a backhoe that is working. We will watch them for as long as he wants. When he was three, we must have watched a crew work for over an hour. Three year olds typically do not sit still doing anything for that long. I mostly watched him observe the backhoes in action. I was ready to leave after ten minutes. That is not my passion. However, he is my passion, and it gave me a chance to hold Marcus on my lap for an hour without interruption. It was a great time. He still remembers us doing that together to this day. He remembers it because it was an area in which he had a high level of interest.

Spending time in your areas of passion are always more enjoyable. Think back to the last activity you did with one of your children. Was it centered on their passions or yours? Again, I am not saying your kids should never be asked to do something they do not enjoy doing. They need to learn to be selfless and put the needs of others first. I am simply sharing my observations of parents who have strong relationships with their children. If you want to have influence with your kids as they get older, then you must invest in them now. Choose to pursue their passions when possible.

2. Model Integrity – I will spend much more time on this topic in the next chapter. I will only briefly mention it here. Parents, we must model integrity for our children. Successful parents do. Throughout fifteen years of teaching, I have spoken with hundreds of teenagers. A common frustration for many of them is that their parents lack integrity. That is their perception. That may not be reality, but their perception is reality to them. Remember, we are beginning with the end in mind. What characteristics do we desire to see from our kids when they are eighteen? Sometimes character traits can by cyclical in nature. If we model integrity for our kids, they may live with it as well. I do know if we choose to live without integrity, we will lose credibility with our children very quickly. This does not bode well for placing yourself in a position of influence. You need to model those traits you desire for them to possess.

3. Have High Standards – The parents who seemingly have strong relationships with their children have high standards or expectations. They are not unrealistic, but they expect certain things from their children. Apparently, these kids are meeting the expectations of their parents. Whenever I was analyzing this information, I was thinking the same thing that many of you are. There are many kids that will not do what is expected of them. In fact, getting some of them to do much of anything can be a challenge.

After researching this concept a little deeper with parents and students, here is my conclusion. These kids met their expectations because their parents value them. The students said they were willing to meet the demands of their parents because they felt like their moms and dads respected, cared for, and loved them unconditionally. Because they knew their parents would never withdraw their love, they were willing to go the extra mile. This is a great position for parents to be in when considering the factor of eighteen.

4. Reward Responsible Behavior – Next door to the house I grew up in, the homeowners took very good care of their lawn. It was soft, very green, and immaculate. They took better care of their grass than anyone I had seen. Because it's true and for the sake of this story, I cannot over emphasize how nice their yard looked. On several occasions, I saw the homeowner chase kids off as they walked through the grass instead of using the sidewalk. It seemed like he had a video camera and monitor that he watched 24/7. As soon as anyone walked across his yard, he was outside prepared for battle.

I can honestly say I was a pretty well-behaved child. I didn't cause much trouble and did my best to walk the straight and narrow. I'm not sure what prompted our actions that night, but two of my friends and I were outside my house playing after returning home from a baseball game. We were eleven or twelve at the time. We had been working on our base running and sliding earlier that week in practice. Sliding is something that most boys enjoy doing. We noticed our neighbor had been watering his yard. He just finished up about the time it was getting dark. The street lights were on and there was a glow in their front yard. Something prompted the three of us to walk across the street and practice our sliding in his front yard. It was a slice of baseball heaven. The yard was wet and soft. It was perfect to practice our sliding. We took turns running down the yard and sliding in the wet grass. We were having so much fun that we didn't notice we were tearing up his front yard. The once perfectly manicured grass was now, well, let's just say destroyed. Once we stopped long enough to observe the damage, we panicked. Our parents found out what we did; then the neighbors found out what we did. They were not pleased at all.

The next day when I saw my two friends at practice, I asked what kind of punishment they received from their parents. One friend was grounded; the other friend got new baseball shoes. When I asked why he got new shoes instead of being punished for tearing up our neighbor's yard, he said, “My parents were proud of me for practicing my sliding.” I couldn't believe it. I knew what we did was wrong. They knew what we did was wrong. Our intentions were innocent. We didn't go there to destroy their yard. We went there to have fun. The destruction was the result of a poor choice, not a willful intent to damage the yard. However, we still deserved to be punished, not rewarded.

Again, I am sharing observations I have learned from other parents who have successful relationships with their children. The lesson to be learned is to reward responsible behavior, not irresponsible behavior. Allow me to paraphrase a quote. What gets rewarded is what gets done. That's why it is important to reward good behavior. Rewarding can be something as small as acknowledging the behavior. As your children get older, you can give more freedom to them when they display responsible behavior. This is a common response I get from students that have great relationships with their parents. They obey their parents and that behavior is rewarded. This is not a situation where the kids manipulate their parents into being rewarded. These parents simply acknowledge the behavior they want to see continue.

Our school even acknowledges a different student each week that chooses to go the extra mile in serving someone else. We want to recognize this type of behavior. There are consequences for poor behavior and rewards for positive behavior. Kids have a tendency to repeat positive behavior when their efforts are appreciated. As kids continue to mature, they can better understand they should do the right thing because it's the right thing to do. For now, we simply want to create these habits and patterns of behavior in their lives. Most of the parents who have solid relationships with their kids recognize, and in some way reward, responsible behavior.

5. Trustworthy – A fifth characteristic I have observed in parents who have a great relationship with their kids is trust. If you have a child who has proven to be untrustworthy, you know the burden it places on your relationship. It creates stress and worry for you, the parent. Is your child where he said he would be? Is he doing something he shouldn't be doing? What is he watching on the television or internet when he is home alone?

In the adult life, it might be a spouse who proves untrustworthy. Maybe it's the boss who promised you the promotion but gave it to someone else. Perhaps it's the friend, whom you confided in, that doesn't keep their promise of confidentiality. Trust is built over time, but can be lost in a fraction of a second. As parents, we certainly do not want to do that to our children. Kids have a great memory when it comes to keeping track of wrongs; they will not forget our broken promises any time soon. You must choose your promises and commitments carefully. Once they are chosen, make sure you keep them. Your children are trusting you to be trustworthy.

The benefits of being trustworthy in the eyes of your children are enormous. Kids are telling me when they feel they can trust their parents, they seek their advice; they ask for their input; they confide in them about their problems; they are more willing to confess their "sins." When my son becomes a teenager, I would much rather he seek advice from his mother or me rather than one of his peers. Building trust with your kids allows you to have influence with them. Remember the importance of beginning with the end in mind. Will the end result look differently if your children trust you? Trust is vitally important in the factor of eighteen.

6. Possess an Attitude of Humility – Sometimes as parents we do and say things out of anger that creates division with our children. Parents that have good relationships with their kids understand this. The way in which you handle this situation will make all the difference in your relationship with your kids. There is a price to pay when we hurt our children. It does impact our relationship with them. That's Relationships 101. Conversations with hundreds of teenagers confirms this for me as well. According to these conversations, kids respect their parents when they have the humility to acknowledge their mistakes. Repentance can be powerful in the eyes of your children. It's also a great characteristic to teach them. Modeling humility for them increases the chances of them possessing it as well.

Again, as a reminder, do not replace accountability with humility. Discipline needs to be consistent and even firm at times. That is a parent's duty. No apology is necessary. However, we are not perfect in parenting. We need to apologize when we make mistakes. It demonstrates humility and compassion. Those are two values we need to teach our children.

I saw this principle in action at Target one day. I was shopping for a birthday card when I heard a mother speaking very firmly to her child. The little girl began crying. Within a few minutes they made their way to my side of the aisle. The mom seemed a little weary. I can only imagine, but I would think taking three young kids shopping with you would be exhausting. When I saw the little girl wiping her tears, I knew she was the one in trouble. She looked about five.

They were close enough that I was able to hear and view their next interaction. The mom leaned over to the little girl and said, "Honey, I am sorry for the way I talked to you. I am very tired, but that gave me no right to speak to you like that. I am very sorry. Will you please forgive me?" The little girl responded with a big smile and said, "I knew you still loved me mommy." They embraced and all was well in her little world. Did you catch it? The mom knew she had mishandled the situation. However, she was humble enough to acknowledge her mistake and ask for forgiveness. Apologize when needed, but make it sincere. Your kids will respect you for it, and you will be modeling a character trait they need to develop in their own life. Successful parents possess and demonstrate humility.

Lessons Learned – No Regrets

Another lesson I learned through conversations with parents of my students is to have no regrets with your children. Allow me to explain it this way.

If I could do it over again what would I do differently? Have you ever been asked that question? In other words, do you have any regrets? I coach basketball and there are times that I look back and wish I could redo something. Maybe I would have changed a game winning play. Maybe I would have switched defenses in a certain situation. You learn from those mistakes and are better prepared for the next time. Usually in sports, there is a next time.

What about with your kids? Any regrets? Would you do anything differently? Would you lighten up a bit more? Would you spend more time with them? Maybe you wouldn't let the little things bother you so much.

Perhaps this is why grandparents are so great. They learned from their mistakes. They can devote all of their time to their grandchildren. If parents could have the wisdom of grandparents, without spoiling the kids, of course, would we be better?

We all have certain regrets in life. Hopefully, how we raise our kids will not be one of those regrets. Fifty parents were interviewed and were asked, "If you had to do it over again, what would you do differently?" This partial list was compiled by Terry Williams in his article "What I Would Have Done Differently."

"Never let my child know that it is even within the realm of possibility to buy ice cream from an ice cream truck."

"I'd work as hard on planning good times for my husband and myself as I do planning them for the children."

"I would have spent more time with them when they were young."

"I wouldn't have put so much energy into my career. After spending time with my son, I've found our relationship is more important than a promotion."

In his book, *Parenting Principles From the Heart of a Pediatrician*, Dr. William Slonecker records these responses from his friend, William Tate, when asked what he would do differently:

"I would spend more time with my children."

"I would not tell them how to do everything. I would let them be creative and do it their way."

"I would build a series of little successes in their lives."

"I would be positive and not critical."

"I would open our home to their friends. They would always feel welcome in our home."

Dr. Slonecker goes on to say, "These are wise words from a grandparent." It's a shame we can't be grandparents first and then a parent."

What you do from here is up to you. Loving your kids, teaching your kids, and spending time with your kids are necessary and desirable investments that will reap great rewards and blessings. Those are the type of things that will build deeper relationships with them. It's very beneficial to build on those moments. Need I remind you that their eighteenth birthday is just around the corner? The final embrace is coming. Never forget the factor of eighteen. When it comes to your children, live with them in such a way that you have no regrets!

Lessons Learned – Value What Your Kids Value

In his book, *The Seven Habits of Highly Effective People,* Stephen Covey tells this story. "I have a friend whose son developed an avid interest in baseball. My friend wasn't interested in baseball at all. But one summer he took his son to see every major league baseball team play one game. The trip took over six weeks and cost a great deal of money, but it became a powerful bonding experience in their relationship. My friend was asked on his return, 'Do you like baseball that much?' 'No, but I like my son that much'." This is a great example of valuing what your kids do. I can only imagine how much influence that had on the son.

My parents were instrumental in my life as well. They were very involved; for that I am grateful. As an adult, I can now better understand the sacrifices my parents made for me. They both worked, my dad two jobs at times. With that said, they were always there at my school events, ball games, birthday parties, and every other event that was important to me.

My dad enjoyed sports a lot, but I know he was tired after work. He was still willing to let me practice my pitching, throw batting practice, or rebound for me while I worked on my jump shot. He valued what I valued. He knew I was passionate about sports and used that as an avenue to continue building a deeper relationship with me. It sent a message to me that my dad cared deeply for me. It built trust. He made huge deposits in my life. My mom took the same approach. She was always very supportive. She came to all my games. She too valued what I valued. From my perspective, it gave them more flexibility in my life to instill those values they wanted me to possess as an adult. I am most grateful for my parents and the sacrifices they made. They set me on a course that gave me the best chance for success.

Chapter 3 thought questions:

1. If experience truly is a great teacher, what lessons have you learned in raising your kids? In other words, what would you continue doing, or not repeat with your next child?
2. Are there any areas you feel you need to raise the standards you have set for your children? If so, what would they be?
3. List the three things you believe your child or children value the most. After writing them down, determine how you can use these to spend quality time with them. How can you use this time to impact the factor of eighteen?

Chapter 4
Stumbling Blocks

My son went through a phase where he enjoyed stringing rope, yarn, and string throughout the house. He tied it around chairs, table legs, door knobs, and anything else he could find. This was normally done when left in the responsible hands of his grandparents.

I arrived home late one night from a basketball game. Little did I know his handy work was still there from earlier in the day. My wife and son were already asleep. I was trying to be quiet so I wouldn't wake them. I thought my phone light was sufficient to see. As I walked through the dining room I saw the rope strung from one end of the room to the other. I noticed it at the very last second. I laughed to myself thinking how disastrous that could have been had I not seen it. I was pretty pleased with my ninja like senses to detect the rope in near darkness. I lowered my phone closer to the maze of rope to see where to step. As I was admiring my Bruce Lee like reflexes I took a step over the rope and onto a strategically placed race car. The weight of my foot placed the wheels in motion and down I went. I felt like a fly in a spider's web. I was twisted in the rope. It took a minute to get myself untangled. I'm sure it would have been an America's Funniest Home Video winning moment.

It was late. I was tired and ready for bed. His maze and race car became a stumbling block slowing me down from achieving my objective of getting to bed as soon as possible.

As we relate this to the factor of eighteen, what are some of the stumbling blocks in the way of your kids? Or, what are the stumbling blocks in your way preventing you from instilling the proper values in the lives of your children? Let me share a few that I have observed.

I briefly mentioned the idea of integrity in a previous chapter. I now want to go in more detail on this topic. I cannot adequately express the importance of integrity. Allow me to give a couple of examples.

King David from the Bible is often referred to as a man after God's own heart. He did a lot of great things, but when I asked students what he is most remembered for; I usually got these two responses: how he defeated Goliath and his affair with Bathsheba. Think about that for a moment. David sacrificed his integrity for a moment, and will always be remembered for that. Let's read the story from 2 Samuel.

2 Samuel 11

David and Bathsheba

1 "In the spring, at the time when kings go off to war, David sent Joab out with the king's men and the whole Israelite army. They destroyed the Ammonites and besieged Rabbah. But David remained in Jerusalem.

*2 One evening David got up from his bed
and walked around on the roof of the palace. From
the roof he saw a woman bathing. The woman was
very beautiful, 3 and David sent someone to find
out about her. The man said, "Isn't this Bathsheba,
the daughter of Eliam and the wife of Uriah the
Hittite?" 4 Then David sent messengers to get her.
She came to him, and he slept with her. (She had
purified herself from her uncleanness.) Then she
went back home. 5 The woman conceived and sent
word to David, saying, "I am pregnant."*

*6 So David sent this word to Joab: "Send
me Uriah the Hittite." And Joab sent him to David.
7 When Uriah came to him, David asked him how
Joab was, how the soldiers were and how the war
was going. 8 Then David said to Uriah, "Go down
to your house and wash your feet." So Uriah left
the palace, and a gift from the king was sent after
him. 9 But Uriah slept at the entrance to the palace
with all his master's servants and did not go down
to his house.*

*10 When David was told, "Uriah did not go
home," he asked him, "Haven't you just come from
a distance? Why didn't you go home?"*

*11 Uriah said to David, "The ark and Israel
and Judah are staying in tents, and my master Joab
and my lord's men are camped in the open fields.
How could I go to my house to eat and drink and
lie with my wife? As surely as you live, I will not do
such a thing!"*

*12 Then David said to him, "Stay here one
more day, and tomorrow I will send you back."*

So Uriah remained in Jerusalem that day and the next. 13 At David's invitation, he ate and drank with him, and David made him drunk. But in the evening Uriah went out to sleep on his mat among his master's servants; he did not go home.

14 In the morning David wrote a letter to Joab and sent it with Uriah. 15 In it he wrote, "Put Uriah in the front line where the fighting is fiercest. Then withdraw from him so he will be struck down and die."

16 So while Joab had the city under siege, he put Uriah at a place where he knew the strongest defenders were. 17 When the men of the city came out and fought against Joab, some of the men in David's army fell; moreover, Uriah the Hittite died.

18 Joab sent David a full account of the battle. 19 He instructed the messenger: "When you have finished giving the king this account of the battle, 20 the king's anger may flare up, and he may ask you, 'Why did you get so close to the city to fight? Didn't you know they would shoot arrows from the wall? 21 Who killed Abimelech son of Jerub-Besheth[b]? Didn't a woman throw an upper millstone on him from the wall, so that he died in Thebez? Why did you get so close to the wall?' If he asks you this, then say to him, 'Also, your servant Uriah the Hittite is dead'."

22 The messenger set out, and when he arrived he told David everything Joab had sent him to say. 23 The messenger said to David, "The men overpowered us and came out against us in the open, but we drove them back to the entrance to the city gate. [24] *Then the archers shot arrows at your servants from the wall, and some of the king's men died. Moreover, your servant Uriah the Hittite is dead."*

What can we observe from this? David has an affair with Bathsheba. He then has Uriah, her husband, brought home to sleep with her. That way Uriah would think the baby was his. However, Uriah refused to stay with his wife. David once again chose to lack integrity in his life by having Uriah placed on the front lines of the battlefield so he would be killed.

How did David find himself in this position? Where was the stumbling block located? Let's look at David and Joseph's situation. Joseph found himself in a similar spot but managed to flee the situation. Let's begin by analyzing David's story first.

What a time to take a stroll on the rooftop. What a moment for some fresh air. He was innocent at this point or was he? Bathsheba was taking a bath on her rooftop. Was this the first time? Was this the first time David saw her taking a bath from his roof? Did she hang out there often and David hoped to catch a glimpse of her? Was this strictly an issue of bad timing and David was captured? Did David instantly turn away when he realized what he was seeing? Maybe he started to walk away, but lust filled his heart and tugged at his sinful nature. So, he did what many of us often do. He traded integrity for gratification.

Joseph was described as a well-built and handsome man. He wasn't a king like David, but held a position that every man holds - he was in charge of his own decisions. Potiphar's wife was beautiful. She would have been a temptation for most men. She wasn't the object of Joseph's affection. She was the pursuer. This undoubtedly increased the temptation for Joseph. There was no fear of rejection if he returned the interest.

David runs to temptation while Joseph flees from it. David gives in while Joseph opts out of it. David's gaze lingers on Bathsheba. Joseph looks away and runs away. If you know the story of David and Bathsheba, you know they have a child together. Bathsheba's husband, Uriah, is off to war. David brings him home to be with his wife, but he refuses. To cover up his sin, David gives orders to have Uriah put on the front lines of the battlefield. Uriah is killed and David takes Bathsheba as his wife. David had to perpetuate the sin in order to cover up his lack of integrity.

Joseph flees the situation and remains faithful to God. We see that he is later rewarded for his choices. What is the difference between these two men? One chooses integrity. One lacks it. Wait a minute! David is described as a man after God's own heart. He must have had integrity. He surely did, but part of having integrity is having it all the time. One mistake doesn't mean you lack integrity. However, one mistake may be what defines you in the eyes of others.

Integrity can be defined as strictly following a moral code. That code will be different for some people. However, God holds us accountable to His standards. David failed to live up to God's standard in this situation. How are you doing? Is integrity important to you? Does it guide your decisions? It needs to. I'm not saying we have to be perfect as parents. But, integrity needs to characterize who we are. Lacking integrity will eventually become a stumbling block in your life. It will either cause you to stumble, leading to a lack of credibility with your children, or it will be a stumbling block in your relationship with your kids. My students don't always live with integrity, but they expect their teachers to model it and rightfully so. Kids will expect the same from their parents. Let me continue to illustrate the importance of integrity with a couple more examples.

It was my freshman year of college. We were a couple of weeks into preseason practices. Our coach had given us a shooting and fundamental workout we had to do at the beginning of each practice. It was what we did every day when we came into the gym. It gave us direction so we wouldn't waste practice time.

Coach was always there to make sure we were doing it right. However, the team walked into practice one day and our coach was not there. We started working on our practice routine. Ten minutes later coach was still not there. Players began asking if anyone knew where he was, but no one knew. We went back to work. About five minutes later coach was still nowhere to be found. It was interesting to watch what happened next - no coach, no accountability, no work ethic. A large number of players stopped their workout and began goofing off. Some of the players began shooting half court shots; others were shooting three point hook shots. Perhaps worst of all, some of the players just quit and sat down on the bench. There were a small handful of us who continued our workout. Fortunately, I was one of them. I hope integrity played a part in my decision, but I can't remember. I know some of my decision to keep working was driven by the fact that I simply wanted to be better. Continuing to work was the right thing to do. I certainly knew that, but so did everyone else. What kept some of us working while the rest stopped? Was it fear? Was it work ethic? Was it integrity? Was it a desire to get better? I'm not totally sure, but I was glad I did. A few minutes later our coach yells from the top of the bleachers. He had been in the sound booth at the top of the gym. The lights in the booth were off and you couldn't see in, but he could see our every move. Players ran back on the court and began shooting instantly. However, it was too late. He had observed enough. Fear fell over that half of the court. He looked at the guys on my half of the court and told us to continue. The other end was a different story. Let's just say it never happened a second time.

What does integrity look like? What does integrity not look like? You would recognize it without a description. No sketch artist is needed.

You wouldn't remember all the faces anyway. You have seen this person next to you in the classroom. You know the one who found it easier to cheat than study. You may have seen this person at your local Walmart. It's the person who finds shoplifting easier than working to pay for something. It's the business owner who cheats on his taxes. It's the husband who is unfaithful to his wife. It's the employee who calls in sick so he can go fishing. People cheat, steal, lie and do a host of other things because they lack the integrity to do the right thing. Most of us have been there. Most of us, if not all of us, have made the wrong decision. If those things give us a picture of what integrity doesn't look like, then what does it look like?

It's the single mom who is struggling to make ends meet but continues tithing faithfully to the church. It's the student who honestly didn't have time to study, but chooses to suffer the consequences of a bad grade instead of cheating. It's the dad or mom who goes to work early to get their work done on time so they can honor their promise of being at their child's game. It's the Internet viewer who stays away from inappropriate websites even though they are home alone.

Integrity helps us make the right choices. Integrity will guide you when you find yourself at a crossroad. It will help you be prepared to make the right choice when facing a moral dilemma. How will you respond when the crisis takes place? Let me illustrate this with a story told by John C. Maxwell. "Some years earlier in Tylenol's mission statement, they had a line saying they would 'operate with honesty and integrity.' Several weeks before the Tylenol incident (someone added cyanide to Tylenol capsules) the president of Johnson and Johnson sent a memo to all presidents of divisions of the company asking if they were abiding by and if they believed in the mission statement. All of the presidents came back with an affirmative answer. Reportedly, within an hour of the Tylenol crisis, the president of the company ordered all capsules off the shelf, knowing it was a $100 million decision. When reporters asked how he could decide so easily and rapidly on such a major decision, his reply was, 'I was practicing what we agreed on in our mission statement'."

Seven people died in the Chicago area as a result of consuming the poisoned Tylenol capsules. Someone had tampered with the medication by adding cyanide. You can picture the upper management now taking Advil to deal with the headache of the Tylenol Crisis. However, as painful as losing $100 million was, it was an easy decision because they knew what they stood for already. Integrity guides you to do the right thing.

When I leave my son alone with my wife, I know she is going to take great care of him because she loves him. Her love mandates her to do the right thing for him. I trust her to do that because she has been consistent in doing what is best for him. Her love mandates her to do the right thing. ***Let me repeat that, her love mandates her to do the right thing.*** Have I made that clear? Your integrity will mandate that you make the right choice. If you have been consistent with making the right choices and displaying integrity in your life, your children will trust you to do the right thing for them. What a great place to be. Again, this gives you influence in their lives. It improves your position of influence. Remember, influence is important in the overall scope of the factor of eighteen. How can you instill those desired traits in their lives if they do not trust you and will not listen to you? You must keep integrity at the forefront of your mind until it becomes who you are.

As a parent or parent to be, have you thought through how you will react or respond to tough situations that are likely to arise? Before you answer that question, let's be very clear about one important component of integrity. You must possess it and live by it before you can hold others accountable to it.

There are some years that my players do not share the same passion for basketball that I do. It usually leads to a long and frustrating year. When a coach invests in his or her program and receives very little return on that investment, it is really discouraging. A coach has to make the decision that he or she is going to continue to coach and work hard regardless of how the team responds. Why? It is the right thing to do. You can't stop working with all your heart just because others do. It's an issue of integrity.

According to a survey of 1,300 Senior Executives, 71% said integrity was the quality most needed to succeed in business. It really is that important. Dwight Eisenhower said it this way: "In order to be a leader, a man must have followers, and to have followers, a man must have their confidence. Hence, the supreme quality for a leader is unquestionably integrity. Without it, no real success is possible, no matter whether it is on a section gang, a football field, in the army, or in an office. If a man's associates find that he lacks forthright integrity, he will fail. His teachings and actions must square with each other. The first great need, therefore, is integrity and high purpose." This is certainly applicable for parents as well. If you want your child to possess integrity, you must model it for him. I came across this comparison of living with integrity versus living without it. This is a paraphrase:

With Integrity:	**Without Integrity:**
Does what is right	Does what is easy
Fights to the end	Quits when difficult
Accepts responsibility	Places blame
Encourages	Discourages
Celebrates teammates' success	Jealous of teammates' success
Has influence	No followers
Trusted by others	Trusted by no one

Seeks to learn	Claims to know
Consistently faithful	Stabs in the back
Brings joy when they show up	Brings joy when they go home

Perhaps you understand integrity is an important component of parenting. However, maybe it is not something you have made a priority at this point; maybe you made that one mistake that you are being remembered for and it is restricting your influence potential. Remove this stumbling block from your life right now. Commit to living with integrity. You might need to seek forgiveness from your children. This could be a powerful moment for you in terms of your influence with your kids. How would they respond if you humbled yourself and went to them confessing your wrongdoing as a parent and asked for a fresh start?

Everyone understands the importance of integrity, but few are willing to live by it. Don't let it be a stumbling block in your life as you continue to try and model this key character quality for your kids.

These next two potential stumbling blocks will not apply to every parent, but I would encourage you to read them anyway. Through coaching, I have seen two areas that have been detrimental to the child/parent relationship. Usually, when these two mistakes are made, they are driven by a strong desire for your child to excel. The intent is harmless, but the result can be devastating.

Stumbling Block – Being a Results Oriented Parent Only

Let me begin with a story that is all too common. I know of a young man who was a very good athlete. He played a few different sports and excelled at each. He worked very hard at developing his skills and was completely dedicated to being the very best athlete possible. When he had a bad performance, he managed to keep things in proper perspective. His parents were a different story. The parents would yell at him. They would ask him how he expected to get a college scholarship with performances like that. They made his life miserable. He wanted to quit sports so he could escape the barrage of insults. However, his love for sports motivated him to continue. The relationship suffered with every performance that did not meet the expectations of his parents.

Many parents become entangled in the star power of their child. This causes them to miss a golden opportunity to use sports as a way to teach life skills and develop a better relationship with their child. Instead, they are only satisfied when their child achieves positive results.

This young man is more concerned about getting out of his parents' house than getting a college diploma. His parents have lost control and are surprisingly confused about how their relationship quickly dissolved. This is the consequence of being a results oriented parent. We all want our children to perform well. We should have high, but realistic expectations for our kids. If they truly are great athletes, then expect great things from them. However, there is a bigger picture to keep in mind. In reference to the parents mentioned above, which do you think they would choose now: for their child to have averaged ten more points per game in high school or to have a better relationship with their child? What is important to you?

Have you made your list of attributes that are important for your child to possess? Again, these are the traits you would like to see by the time they are eighteen. Remember, if the well-being of your child at the age of eighteen is important, then that will dictate how you act toward them today. What are some of those character traits you desire for them? Once you have determined that list you can use it as a gauge. At the end of each day you can use that list as a framework to determine whether or not you are modeling those traits for your child. Then you can ask yourself if your words and actions directed toward your child are building toward that list or a completely different list. If parents are not willing to work at this, then we cannot expect our children to possess these qualities.

How can sports help in this process? As you can see from above, if you are a results oriented parent, things are great as long as your child is producing results. What happens when you become frustrated during the time he or she is not performing up to his or her potential? My experience in coaching has led me to believe this creates kids who resent their parents' involvement in their sports. Unfortunately, the parents begin to carry this critical spirit over to other areas of their child's life. This only intensifies the situation because it happens more often now.

I am a coach who trains my athletes to perform and win. I want to win as much as anyone. However, I also understand there are games we can't win. There are teams that we simply cannot beat. If you measure your success on winning only, there will be a lot of frustrating nights. There are other ways of measuring success. Did we perform better in our areas of weakness? Did we perform better than the last time we played this team? Is our scoring average increasing? Are we allowing fewer points per game? How was our effort? Did we communicate collectively as a team? These are all measurable things to indicate if we are improving. You can do the same with your child. They will have a bad game. They might get in a rut and have several bad games. Instead of letting this frustrate you to the point of impacting your relationship, look for opportunities to teach life skills. Think about your list of traits you want your child to develop. Teach your child that while they may have a bad game, they can still maintain a high work ethic. They can still perform with a positive attitude. They can contribute to the team by encouraging their teammates, even when they are performing poorly. That takes mental toughness. They would be learning how to work hard, how to have a great attitude in difficult circumstances, how to be a team player and becoming mentally tough. What employer wouldn't want those traits in their employees? Again, what is the end result you desire from your kids? There are so many life skills to be learned through sports. Teach your child to win. Teach your child to want to win. Teach your child what it takes to win. However, in that process, they need to know you care more about them as a person than the kind of results they produce as a player.

Learning to win and learning life skills are not mutually exclusive. You can have the best of both worlds. However, keep things in their proper perspective. You don't want your child to resent you. Resentment is certainly a relational stumbling block.

Stumbling Block – Sports and Bad Timing

As I stated earlier, this book is not meant to provide a systematic or progressive approach. It is meant to be practical and applicable. These are simply observations that hinder or help in the process of instilling the proper values in your children by the time they are eighteen.

The next stumbling block is hard to prevent and even more difficult to overcome. I simply call it sports and poor timing.

Have you ever had a bad day at work where nothing goes right? You are late to work because of traffic. Your computer doesn't work once you get to work. Your report gets turned in late as a result of the computer issue. Now your boss is angry because your report is late. You survive until lunch time. You think you have enjoyed a relaxing lunch until you look down and realize your hamburger leaked every possible condiment ever invented. Now your shirt has an additional six colors that were not there prior to lunch. You get back to work and find the president of the company wants to discuss your report. He doesn't seem to care for your report or the lunch stains on your shirt. By the end of the day, you are tired, stressed, angry, confused, and ready to be home. The ride home only adds to your stress because you get behind the only guy who wants to drive 15 mph in a 45 mph speed zone. You finally arrive home and walk in the door. Your spouse is awaiting your arrival. You are expecting a welcome home hug and a how was your day question. However, the first words out of his or her mouth are, "The car has a flat tire. I thought you were taking out the trash this morning," or some other annoying comment. What they said wasn't annoying because of the comment itself. It was annoying because of bad timing.

If your wife or husband had a clue what kind of day you just had, they wouldn't have said that to you at that moment. Do we ever do similar things to our children; maybe after they perform poorly at a game? Remember, it isn't always what we say, but when we say it.

Bad timing can destroy an opportunity for a constructive conversation. This becomes incredibly important if you already have a strained relationship with your child.

Here is how I see this play out in the sports arena. The parents watch their kid play in a game.

Maybe the child has a bad performance. He didn't shoot well. She had too many turnovers. He struck out every time at bat. She missed her serve in volleyball. Whatever sport they play, they certainly have had a bad game or two over the years. The parents watch the game and become increasingly frustrated as the game progresses because their child is not performing well. The child walks out of the locker room and mopes over to their parents. They dread the ride home because they know their parents are going to be critical. By the time they get home the parents have more than frustrated their child and the child has been very disrespectful to their parents. Can you relate to this? Can you prevent this? You may have a great relationship with your child, but it takes a turn for the worse after every game. If you could just fix this aspect of your relationship, it would be perfect. Or, you have a seriously strained relationship already and sports seem to drive the wedge of separation even deeper. There is hope and it is a simple solution.

Many schools have adopted a policy for parents to follow when talking to a coach. If the parent is unhappy with their child's coach, they are not allowed to speak to the coach about it for twenty-four hours. Emotions are the highest immediately following a game. That is not a good time for parents to confront a coach. Both sides may be upset and this can lead to a break down in what should be a professional conversation. If adults cannot always control their temper when emotions are high, can we really expect sixteen year old kids to do that?

May I suggest the following solutions? First, do not be critical of your child's performance, especially right after the game. They know they played badly. They don't need anyone to tell them. Chances are, they just listened to their coach indicate the same thing. Walking out to their parents should be a place of refuge, not a place of contention.

Secondly, learn to ask the proper questions. You can check your child's comprehension of their performance by getting feedback instead of giving criticism. Wait for enough time to pass so their emotions have settled down a little. Then make a positive comment to lead into your question. For example, you played great defense in your game tonight. How do you think you played? They will usually respond in one of two ways. "I don't want to talk about it right now." There is your clue. Let it go at this point. Getting your point across is not worth straining your relationship. The second thing is they may begin to list out all of the things they did wrong. This gives you permission to continue your questioning. "What do you think caused those problems tonight? Do you feel like giving me an example of what you mean? Is there anything you would do differently in your preparation to prevent this from happening in the next game?" I would encourage you to finish on a positive note at the end of your conversation. "I know you feel like you really struggled in your game, but I really liked the way you were mentally tough enough to play great defense." This reminds them that you noticed something positive. Let them hear encouragement first. This may open the door for some constructive criticism later.

I interviewed almost 100 athletes. Forty-six percent said they do not listen to their parents' advice when it comes to sports. I think that is an inappropriate response for kids to take. However, it is the hard truth. If this is the case, we as parents need to be aware that our kids may not always want our advice. If this is true for your kid, then you have to ask yourself the following question. Would I rather make my point or improve my relationship with my child? If your child allows you to discuss their performance, remember not to have bad timing and learn to ask good questions rather than being critical. This can be the difference between building a healthy relationship or ruining your child's passion for the game. Or worse, it can damage your credibility. Remember the factor of eighteen. We are trying to funnel our kids in the right direction. If we continually do things to weaken our relationship, they will turn to someone else for guidance. That may not always be a good thing. Remember the big picture, and do things that will increase your influence in their lives.

Stumbling Block – Absenteeism

The next stumbling block that can and will likely hinder the factor of eighteen is absenteeism. More and more children are being raised in single parent homes, or where one or both parents are gone so often they have no positive impact on their children. Please don't misunderstand me. I know several single parents who are doing tremendous jobs and love their children as much as anyone. I also understand the need for both parents to work in today's market. It becomes an issue when neither parent is there when kids arrive home from school. If the parents are not there, then something else becomes the influence in the child's life. Television, computers, phones, video games, and bad friends all make the list of things that can potentially steer your child down the wrong path. The closer your child gets to eighteen, the more critical these outside influences become. Let's say your child is sixteen. If they choose the wrong crowd and are led down the wrong path, you have far less time to help them recover before they turn eighteen. By the way, there is nothing special about the age of eighteen. I have used this as a landing point due to the beginning of college for most eighteen year olds. This is simply the time where many will leave home for school. At this point, you have either instilled the values or you have not.

Unfortunately, there are several things not being taught to our youth today. As I teach and counsel approximately 150 teens each year, I am finding the power of influence parents actually have. This can obviously be a great thing or a very detrimental thing. Contrary to common belief, youth really are listening to their parents. Parents, you have more influence in your child's life than you might realize. They want parents who are in control. They want parents who can offer wisdom and advice. However, you need to be aware there is a delicate balance between being there for your kids and being too controlling, at least from their perspective. I am discovering through conversations with youth that many parents have an incorrect perception that when their kids hit the teenage years, they don't want to be around their parents anymore. This is actually not the case, if you have a healthy relationship. Teens will certainly begin to desire more freedom and time spent with their friends. However, this should not be interpreted that they do not want you involved in their lives; this is simply a transitional time for them. Parents, this is not the time to abandon them. They expect you to be their parents. They want you to be their parents. They need your wisdom and guidance more than ever. They will not likely verbalize those thoughts, but that is the message being sent to me loud and clear from the vast majority of teenagers I speak with each year.

If you are experiencing just the opposite, and your child is beginning to pull away from you, this can be a sign of a problem in your relationship.

One of the biggest frustrations kids are sharing with me is that if a parent has been absent for most of their lives, why do they think they can have power and influence now? If you have been an absent parent, it can be fixed, but understand it will take time. You must get busy because you are running out of time. How do you fix this? Remember these three R's - Repentance, reconciliation, and return.

Repentance - This is such a powerful and humbling event. To repent requires admission of guilt. This is a difficult but powerful step. You must be sincere with your child. If they sense this is simply a way to manipulate them, they will withdraw or become angry. Humble yourself and truly repent. Seek their forgiveness. You don't have to be weak, just be honest and open with them. Tell them you have not been there at the level you should have been, but you want to change from this point forward. It will take time to prove this to them. Be patient but remain committed.

Reconciliation – Some of the responses I have received from youth who have experienced the absentee parent are not always favorable. Reconciliation will not be easy most of the time. It too will require patience. You will have to regain their trust and respect. Again, spend time with them in their areas of interest and passion. See things from their perspective, but continue to provide discipline and require respect.

Return – Return to being the best parent you can be. Engage in the whole process of being their parent. Be there for them. Go to their recitals, practices, and games. Don't allow less important things in your life to crowd out time with your kids. This will require one hundred percent effort. The factor of eighteen demands you do this. It's about influencing your children to make the best possible decisions they can make to set their lives on the right path.

I mentioned the good news is that kids want their parents involved at some level. The down side is that if parents are not involved, kids will turn to someone or something else. You get to make that choice of whom or what will influence your kids. Absenteeism is not an option in the factor of eighteen.

There are several qualities not being passed on to our children due to absent parents, especially fathers. One key characteristic I see missing is leadership. Many kids are not being taught how to be leaders. Because of this, we are raising a generation of followers. If parents are not leading, and their kids are followers, then we must ask whom are they following? That scares me in today's culture. Let's look again to the life of David. He demonstrated great leadership and strength of character in this area of his life. Let's examine his life and see what we can learn about leadership.

David was the youngest of eight boys. I'm sure his shepherd position seemed unimportant to him at times. His three oldest brothers were off to war. I'm guessing David had plenty of time to reflect while tending the sheep. "If only I were older. I wish I could trade the sheep field for the battle field."

Jesse, his father, sent David to deliver some food to his brothers and see how they were doing. This trip would not only change his life, but would also become one of the best known stories in the

Bible. David took on a tall order and he didn't come up on the short end of the deal.

Goliath was over nine feet tall. David was a mere boy. The scene looked much like a bully picking on the under-sized boy at the play ground. No one expected the fight to last long. They were all correct. David cut him down to size; let's just say Goliath was at least a head shorter after the fight.

David's father told him to take some food to his brothers and then report how they were doing. David arrives on the scene to find this giant defying the Israelites. The Israelites would run in fear every time Goliath came out to fight. Instead of a huge battle taking place, the concept was for one soldier from each army to fight. The army that was represented by the losing soldier would become subject to the other army.

David was not going to tolerate this giant defying the army of God. The problem appeared to be that David could do nothing about the situation. It would be like a six year old boy getting mad at his twelve year old brother. You can get as angry as you want, but when push comes to shove, the twelve year old is going to take down his younger brother every time. The soldiers were probably not taking him seriously at first. His brothers were simply annoyed at David. The problem was that this was not a simple argument between two brothers. This was not even a grade school bully pushing around a weaker kid. This was a fight in which most observers expected David to be killed.

So, what prompted David to fight Goliath under such difficult odds?

I believe David's response was prompted by at least three things:

1. The absence of leadership. He saw that no one else was going to do it. Those who were seemingly more capable ran the other direction. They had forty days in which they could have fought Goliath. If they were going to do it, they would have done it by now. David shows up and is prepared on day one.

2. His faith in God's power. Sincere faith in God will prompt a person to action.

3. His confidence in his ability and preparation.

I often wonder how much of this was complete faith in God and how much was confidence in his own ability. Have you ever been in that position? You trust God, but not your own ability. Who wins, God's power or your weakness? Maybe you do not even believe in God and are left depending solely on your own ability. What happens when your ability comes up short? Are you scared to try the same thing next time because you cannot do it?

I remember when I was in the seventh grade. It was the first day of Jr. High school for me. I have no musical ability at all, but have always enjoyed sports and been fairly successful. I had enrolled in P.E. class, but the schedule listed me in choir class. Choir class was the last thing I would have signed up for. I cannot even come close to making a joyful noise unto the Lord. However, I didn't panic when I saw my schedule. I had been going to school long enough that I knew the first day of school routine by then. The teacher would have the usual class introductions, hand out the syllabus, and go over the class rules and expectations. I knew this would take up the entire hour. As soon as class was over I would go straight to the office and get my schedule changed and everything would be just fine, right? Wrong! There were no class introductions. There was no passing out the class syllabus. There was no mention of class rules. The teacher walks in and tells us to have a seat on the risers.

Then he said that he wanted to hear us sing. My heart sped up a little, but not too much as I thought I could get lost in the crowd and not be heard. No such luck. The teacher announced he would call us up one by one for solos in front of the class. You have got to be kidding me. What kind of music teacher makes students sing a solo on the first day of school? Isn't junior high school awkward enough already. I began to panic, my palms were sweating, and my heart was racing. I had placed myself in the middle of the group on the risers. I was in a pretty good position. If he started on the bottom row and went from left to right working his way up the risers person by person, I stood a strong chance of not getting called on to sing that first day. If I could just survive day one, I would change my schedule and be gone from his class forever. Again, no such luck. He called us to the front in alphabetical order. I was in big trouble now. With a last name that begins with the letter "B" I knew I would have to face the firing squad that day. I was confident there would be at least one or two students called before my turn came. This would give me a few minutes to think of a way out of this musical fiasco. In case you are wondering what the big deal is, did I tell you I cannot sing at all? I am beyond terrible. The next thing I hear is this, "Blankenship, you're up, let's go." You have got to be kidding me. There must have been at least fifty students in the class; Blankenship is the first name on your list? How I was wishing my mom had married Mr. Zenski. No, I have no idea who that is, but his last name started with a Z and not a B. I quietly stepped up to the piano where the teacher was. I told him that my schedule was incorrect and I was supposed to be in P.E. He said, "That's okay, let's hear you sing anyway." You don't understand. I will not be in here tomorrow. I will be in P.E. class. He said, "I understand but please sing anyway." I finally said, "I can't sing at all. I have a terrible voice." "Let me be the judge of that, now start singing." So, I took a deep breath and waited for him to begin playing. I began singing. He stopped and told me to sing louder. There was no way out at this point. I sang louder and the students began laughing. After a few lines of the song, he stopped and so did I. He looked at me and in front of the entire class and said, "You are right. You can't sing at all. Go back to your spot." It was the worst first day of school ever. I can laugh at it now and have a good story to tell.

Here's my point in telling the story. I knew God could grant me the ability to sing well if He chose to in that moment. I just didn't know if He would or not. I knew trusting in my own musical talent wasn't going to get the job done. If this would have been shooting free throws or hitting a baseball, I would have been fine with that. However, it was singing and I knew I was not gifted in that area. So, what about David's situation? He might have known God could have helped him slay the giant. But, would he have gone out there if he was not well prepared to sling a stone? Was this complete faith in God? Was this complete faith in his own ability? Was this a combination of faith in God and his own ability? I think David possessed great faith in God. However, I think he had spent time preparing himself with the sling. I don't think it was any accident that David killed Goliath. I think his faith in God gave him the courage to go out and execute his skill that he had developed through practice.

Preparation is so vital in being successful. What if David had said to Goliath, give me two months to practice and I will come back? Obviously, that would not have worked. This is why it is so important to always display integrity in your work ethic. You always work hard. You always do your best. You never know when you will be called upon to fight the giant.

David walked up to the battle line. He saw and heard Goliath defying Israel's army. There was no existing leadership with the courage to step up and take charge. So, David trusted God and went out and killed Goliath. David was young. This was not his battle. Others were more qualified, maybe! It was certainly not David's fight, but when no one else would, he did.

Leaders are needed in schools, in the job market, in the church, and certainly in the home. Teaching your kids to be a leader is such a great gift. It will serve them well for life. Leadership is a common trait missing in kids where parental absenteeism is prevalent. This is an observation as well as a stated fact by many teenagers. A high school student shared with me that he did not have a father or a positive male role model in his life; as a result, he doesn't understand how to be a man of God or a leader for his younger sister. This is one of many examples that could be shared.

Parents, let me remind you that I am only sharing traits of successful parent/child relationships that I have observed after teaching for several years. Of course, this is also information that some of the youth I work with are sharing with me as well. My son is too young for me to claim any expert parenting advice at this point. However, along with the observations, much of this is just common sense. You can choose to do what you want with this information. However, I can honestly say that leadership really is a characteristic that is missing from many of our youth today. This is information I have gathered from teaching, speaking to youth groups, visiting with other coaches and teachers. Remember, this is about the absentee parent. If you are not involved in your child's life, it will be very difficult to teach them how to be a leader and make wise, godly decisions. I know life can be difficult. Things happen that are out of our control. With that said, we must fight for our children. We must make them a priority and be involved in their lives. That is our role as their parents.

Chapter 4 Thought Questions

1. For whatever reason, if you have not been involved in your child's life to the level you need to be, how has it impacted your relationship?
2. When considering the factor of eighteen, what character traits do you see missing from your child's life that you would like them to possess by the time they turn 18?
3. What can you restructure in your life to spend more time with your children?
4. If nothing changes in terms of your relationship with your kids, what are the short and long term affects on them?
5. What stumbling blocks are hindering a deeper relationship with your child?

Chapter 5
Key Ingredients

I'm not much of a cook, but I do understand the need to follow a recipe. Some ingredients are not that important. You can leave them out and whatever you are cooking will taste just fine. Other foods can be a different story. Too much or not enough of a certain ingredient will change the taste drastically.

A friend of mine was baking a cake and wasn't thinking clearly. The recipe called for an eighth cup of flour. Well, apparently her math skills were not up to par that day. She added one fourth and one fourth to achieve her eighth cup. The cake was unfit to eat.

Here's my point: I don't think there is a magical recipe in raising kids. All kids are different. You can leave out certain things and the child still turns out great. What I am about to share is not a complete recipe in achieving the desired results in the factor of eighteen. However, after fifteen years of teaching and coaching, these are the factors that are prevalent in nearly all highly successful and positive parent/child relationships. As I look at students and athletes who have the best relationships with their parents, these are some common traits I see from the parents. Add these key ingredients to those found in chapter three and you have a powerful combination of proven suggestions that will significantly help you in the factor of eighteen.

1. Unconditional love – This seems like a no brainer. In fact, most if not all parents will verbally express they love their kids. However, do their actions reflect that? You might be surprised how many times I have seen poor grades and poor sports performances impact relationships. It's not that parents stop loving their kids for bad performances, but rather withdraw their support and praise. If your children are not doing well in school and they are capable of it, please hold them accountable. I'm talking about extreme responses that leaves your children feeling unloved or their emotional tank empty. Having spoken with many teenagers that have great relationships with their parents, uncondtional love was at the top of the list of things they experienced from their parents. When I asked them to define unconditional love for me, this was a common response. "There's nothing we could do or not do to make our parents stop loving us."

2. Integrity – I have spent a lot of time discussing integrity in this book. I won't be redundant here. Just understand that what you say and how you live your life must be consistent with each other. Our children are far more observant than we sometimes realize. Lacking integrity will diminish, if not destroy, your ability to impact

your children for the future. If they do not trust and respect you, they will not listen to you. You will not be able to achieve your desired outcome in the factor of eighteen if you lack integrity. Choose to live with integrity, and you will reap the benefits of having a high level of influence with your children.

3. A balance between accountability and freedom – This is a difficult item to describe because the level of accountability and freedom varies from family to family. The delicate balance for parents is remaining involved in their children's lives without diminishing their freedom. As the level of trust increases, so does the level of freedom. However, one area of freedom that needs to be closely guarded by parents is the selection of friends their children make. Unfortunately, this is a hyper sensitive issue with many youth. Some kids simply do not have the maturity or experience to understand the effects of peer pressure. Parents, we are often instructed to choose our battles with our children. This is one battle I would strongly encourage you to choose. One bad friend is enough to cause your child to go down the wrong path. It only takes one poor decision to alter the course of your child's life. Telling your kids they cannot hang out with certain friends will cause strife. Prepare yourselves for it. However, you must take a stand on this issue. Trust your judgment as a parent. Follow your instinct on this one.

At the very least, monitor the relationship with any questionable friends. That decision could potentially save you and your children a life time of heartache. Here are a couple of Proverbs to substantiate this. Proverbs 13:20 – "*He who walks with the wise grows wise, but a companion of fools suffers harm.*" Proverbs 22:24-25 – "*Do not make friends with a hot-tempered man, do not associate with one easily angered, or you may learn his ways and get yourself ensnared.*"

Key Ingredient - You Have to Get Through

May 22, 2011 is a day that will not be forgotten in the history of Joplin, Missouri. Many of you will remember the EF 5 Tornado that destroyed much of the town. Perhaps some of you reading this even experienced it. I live just north of the area. It was a Sunday afternoon. My wife and I were home with our son working on our lesson plans for the next week of school. The tornado sirens sounded and we did what we normally do when this happens. My wife continued her work and I stepped out on the porch. I know, not the brightest move. However, living in southwest Missouri, we have become accustomed to hearing the tornado sirens with no apparent impending danger. I didn't see much to cause any alarm this time either. I went back inside and turned on the television. The local news station's camera was pointing to the west. Viewing that picture changed my perspective. They were emphatically stressing the importance of taking cover as a large tornado was bearing down on Joplin.

We had a small amount of hail and light wind at the time; so we went to our hallway and waited there. Nothing really ever materialized where we live. However, as we listened to the radio, we heard some really devastating announcements. The person on the radio yelled, "Sonic is gone, Chick-fil-a is destroyed, and Home Depot has been leveled." We began to panic a little at this point. This was the vicinity where my wife's parents lived. We immediately called, but there was no answer. We were obviously concerned but really had no comprehension of the destruction at this point. My wife told me, "You have to go check on my parents!"

I went as soon as the storm passed. My dad, who lives next door to me, went with me. We drove around for the longest time trying to find a passable road to their house. Every road we went down was blocked by fallen trees and other debris. It was impossible to get there. Much of the time I wasn't even sure where we were. Every landmark and road sign I was accustomed to was gone. My dad had recently undergone a knee replacement surgery and was not able to walk well at that point. We turned around and went back home. My plan was to drop my dad off and try a second time. I thought I could get as close as possible and walk the rest of the way.

My wife heard us pull in the driveway and came out to see her parents. She was not pleased when they were not with us. I told her we could not get through because all the roads were blocked. Having no idea of the destruction that was on the roadways, she had no understanding of why we could not get there. Before I could tell her I was going back out, she emphatically told me, "You have to get through to them!" Her statement to me was driven by her love and concern for her parents. I was able to find a route to their house. Their house was destroyed, but thank God both of them were okay.

Here's my point in telling the story. My wife and I were very concerned about her parents. My wife told me, "You have to get through to them" with more emphasis than anything she has told me in the past.

Parents, listen to me. Whatever it takes, no matter how much time it requires, no matter how many sacrifices you make, you have to get through to your children. Their future depends on it. If we become as passionate about getting through to our children as my wife was about me getting through to her parents, we might find ourselves in a better position with them.

I have discussed in detail the importance of being there for your children. If we have no significant relationship with them and very little credibility, we cannot possibly influence the factor of eighteen.

We live in a fallen world. Life is seldom perfect and sometimes extremely difficult. Life gets hard, marriage can be challenging, finances can look bleak, and raising children can be exhausting. Sometimes the only escape seems to be walking away from everything. Our culture has made this all too easy and available. However, everything I read, and young people I talk to from these situations indicate that they are suffering for it. We have to fight for our marriages. We have to work through our problems. Let's face it; divorce can leave a lasting imprint on the lives of our children. I know this is a delicate subject. I know this might sound insensitive. Please know that's not my intent. But I am speaking up for our children. I have seen and heard their pain.

I want to share some statistics as it relates to parents being involved in their children's lives. This is especially true for fathers.

- *"According to the U.S. Census Bureau, 24 million children in America -- one out of three -- live in biological father-absent homes."*

- *"Children in father-absent homes are five times more likely to be poor. In 2002, 7.8 percent of children in married-couple families were living in poverty, compared to 38.4 percent of children in female-householder families. Source: U.S. Census Bureau, Children's Living Arrangements and Characteristics:*

March 2002, P200-547, Table C8. Washington D.C.: GPO, 2003.

- *A child with a nonresident father is 54 percent more likely to be poorer than his or her father. Source: Sorenson, Elaine and Chava Zibman. "Getting to Know Poor Fathers Who Do Not Pay Child Support." Social Service Review 75 (September 2001): 420-434."*

- *"Youths in father-absent households still had significantly higher odds of incarceration than those in mother-father families. Youths who never had a father in the household experienced the highest odds. Source: Harper, Cynthia C. and Sara S. McLanahan. "Father Absence and Youth Incarceration." Journal of Research on Adolescence 14 (September 2004): 369-397.*

- *A 2002 Department of Justice survey of 7,000 inmates revealed that 39% of jail inmates lived in mother-only households. Approximately forty-six percent of jail inmates in 2002 had a previously incarcerated family member. One-fifth experienced a father in prison or jail."*

- *Adolescents, particularly boys, in single-parent families were at higher risk of status, property and person delinquencies. More-*

over, students attending schools with a high proportion of children of single parents are also at risk. Source: Anderson, Amy L. "Individual and contextual influences on delinquency: the role of the single-parent family." Journal of Criminal Justice 30 (November 2002): 575-587.

- *There is significantly more drug use among children who do not live with their mother and father. Source: Hoffmann, John P. "The Community Context of Family Structure and Adolescent Drug Use." Journal of Marriage and Family 64 (May 2002): 314-330.*

- *Youths are more at risk of first substance use without a highly involved father. Each unit increase in father involvement is associated with 1% reduction in substance use. Living in an intact family also decreases the risk of first substance use. Source: Bronte-Tinkew, Jacinta, Kristin A. Moore, Randolph C. Capps, and Jonathan Zaff. "The influence of father involvement on youth risk behaviors among adolescents: A comparison of native-born and immigrant families." Article in Press. Social Science Research December 2004.*

- *Of the 228 students studied, those from single-parent families reported higher rates of drinking and smoking as well as higher scores on delinquency and aggression tests when compared to boys from two-parent households. Source: Griffin, Kenneth W., Gilbert J. Botvin, Lawrence M. Scheier, Tracy Diaz and Nicole L. Miller. "Parenting Practices as Predictors of Substance Use, Delinquency, and Aggression Among Urban Minority Youth: Moderating Effects of Family Structure and Gender." Psychology of Addictive Behaviors 14 (June 2000): 174-184.*

- *In a study of INTERPOL crime statistics of 39 countries, it was found that single parenthood ratios were strongly correlated with violent crimes. This was not true 18 years ago. Source: Barber, Nigel. "Single Parenthood As a Predictor of Cross-National Variation in Violent Crime." Cross-Cultural Research 38 (November 2004): 343-358."*

- *"Researchers at Columbia University found that children living in a two-parent household with a poor relationship with their father are 68% more likely to smoke, drink, or use drugs compared to all teens in two-parent households. Teens in single mother households are at a 30% higher risk than those in two-parent households. Source: "Survey Links Teen Drug Use, Relationship*

With Father." Alcoholism & Drug Abuse Weekly 6 September 1999: 5.

- *Even after controlling for community context, there is significantly more drug use among children who do not live with their mother and father. Source: Hoffmann, John P. "The Community Context of Family Structure and Adolescent Drug Use." Journal of Marriage and Family 64 (May 2002): 314-330.*

- *In a study of 6,500 children from the ADDHEALTH database, father closeness was negatively correlated with the number of a child's friends who smoke, drink, and smoke marijuana. Closeness was also correlated with a child's use of alcohol, cigarettes, and hard drugs and was connected to family structure. Intact families ranked higher on father closeness than single-parent families. Source: National Fatherhood Initiative. "Family Structure, Father Closeness, & Drug Abuse." Gaithersburg, MD: National Fatherhood Initiative, 2004: 20-22.*

If you are a single parent, I want you to know I have the deepest respect and admiration for you. I do not know how you do it alone. My wife and I only have one child. So far he has been easy to raise. However, with work and other responsibilities, it can still be exhausting to raise one child. You deserve a lot of credit for doing it by yourself. Your child needs you. Keep up the good work.

Some of you are in the position you are in due to poor decisions your spouse made. They chose to leave. They chose to neglect their parental responsibilities. Please don't feel beaten down by those statistics. However, please understand that statistically speaking, it does put your children at greater risk.

The good news is that statistics are showing you can improve your child's chances of staying on the straight and narrow path by finding a mentor for them. I would highly recommend the book *Cultivate.* It is by Dr. Jeff Myers with Paul and Paige Gutacker. This is an excellent book on mentoring. Josh and Sean McDowell wrote the foreword and said this, "The hearts of young adults are our treasure, and *Cultivate* is the treasure map." Consider the following from this great book.

"Not surprisingly, new research is confirming what Scripture has already shown us about the significance of life-on-life relationship. In his recently completed doctoral dissertation at Talbot School of Theology, Jason Lanker demonstrated that adolescents who had natural mentors ('relationships with non-parental adults from whom high school students received support and guidance without the help of a formalized program') more deeply experienced God's presence, connected to God in times of suffering, felt realistically accepted

by God and were secure in their relationships with Him.

The study showed that it was not how long they had been Christian or how well their parents had modeled the Christian faith. Rather, it was the fact that they had mentors."

Studies show that more than one-third of American kids do not have their biological father in the home. The National Research Council shares that one out of every four adolescents in America is currently in jeopardy of not achieving a productive adulthood. Education writer Jamie Littlefield says that there are 14.6 million children in America at risk even though the evidence concludes that life-on-life mentoring works.

You can overcome the effects of having one parent absent. You need to find a person (make it the right person) who will be a mentor and role model for your child. If you are a wife or husband and have a strong marriage and relationship with your kids, I would encourage and challenge you to step out and mentor young kids.

I asked Marcus Moeller, a former student of mine, to share his personal story of having a mentor in his life. I am leaving his story unedited.

"Joe and I met in 5th grade. While attending the same school and playing on a basketball team together, we realized we had something in common that really bonded us together: we both LOVED college basketball. The first time Joe and I hung out beyond the walls of our school and the lines of a basketball court was a time I invited myself to

Joe's house to watch Duke vs. North Carolina play another great installment of one of sport's greatest rivalries. My mom explained on many occasions how rude it was to invite yourself to other people's house. Somehow I justified the UNC/Duke rivalry as the exception to this rule and dove head first into an attempt to get to Joe's house to watch this game. However, my intentions were not simply to strike up a new friendship with someone who loved college basketball. You see, in the single parented Moeller household, cable was a luxury we simply couldn't afford. So, on one hand, I was excited to get to know Joe, but on the other, I was going to do anything within my power to find a TV showing my Tarheels take on their heated rival from Durham. I don't know who ended up winning that game, but I do know what came from that night at Joe's house forever changed my life. It didn't take long that evening to find out that Joe's love for college basketball came from his father, Dwaine. I had never been around an older male who loved college basketball as much as I did. It was an obsession for me growing up, and I loved the passion with which Dwaine cheered and yelled at the officials. I was immediately attracted by his kind heart and competitive spirit. It became obvious that night I wanted to be around Joe and Dwaine whenever possible. The more I was around Joe, the more I wanted to be around him and we quickly became inseparable brothers. Dwaine's job description, as it applied to my life, looked something like this: dentist, coach, chauffeur, boat driver, cheerleader, and small group leader. Simply put, Dwaine was my mentor. I am a firm believer that service and action are huge parts of mentoring. Dwaine lived that out every day. When I needed a father figure, Dwaine was there. When I needed to be chastised, Dwaine was there. When I needed someone to listen, Dwaine was there. When I needed to be praised, Dwaine was there. When I needed advice, Dwaine was there. Dwaine was always there. Great teachers have a way of inspiring their pupils to love what they love. As a basketball coach, there are few things as rewarding as having a player decide they want to be a coach after playing for you. The best example of this idea is found in the person of Jesus Christ. I say that not to get a sticker in Sunday School, but because it is the truth. In Matthew 4 Jesus begins the process of calling the 12 disciples. Simon and Andrew were told, "Come, follow me and I will make you fishers of men." Jesus was going to show them His heart for men, and inspire them to take up the torch for His mission when He was gone. After calling the 12 to follow Him, and gathered them all together and He gave us what we find in Matthew 28. In The Great Commission Jesus said, "Therefore, go and make disciples of all nations, baptizing them in the name of the Father, the Son, and the Holy Spirit, and teaching them to obey everything I have commanded you." Jesus was mentoring these 12 men. Dwaine helped me love what he loves. He has a desire to mentor and play a role in the maturation of young people who need guidance and direction. Coaching is a

profession chalked full of numerous mentoring opportunities. Coaching is about far more than winning and losing. For me, it is a mentorship. It is an opportunity to take all of the years of having people like Dwaine pour into me, and do the same for young people in similar situations. I am quite confident that one of the biggest reasons I am where I am today is Dwaine chose to be intentional and mentor me. My goal is to do the same for others."
Marcus Moeller

Having a mentor in your children's lives can be one of the greatest decisions you make for them. It's good to have someone else they respect and admire involved at some level. It's important to have someone partner with you who will help hold them accountable. They will eventually turn to someone. Why not let it be someone you choose to have in their lives that will lead them in the same direction you want them to go. Choose someone who will support the factor of eighteen. That's what Dwaine did for Marcus. Marcus turned out to be a great young man who is walking on the right path in life. He is a great example of the factor of eighteen.

It's sad I have to mention this, however, I must. We live in a dangerous culture. If you mentor someone, here are a few tips to follow to protect yourself. Most of these are common sense, but bear mentioning anyway.

1. Respect the feelings of the parents. Mentoring is a great thing to do. However, it must

be done under the desires of the parent(s). You need to contact the parents and seek their permission. It may be they are the ones who seek you first, but respect them enough to visit with them about your desire to help their child.

2. Stay above reproach. Generally speaking, males should mentor males and females mentor females. An exception would be to include your spouse in the mentoring process. Don't discuss inappropriate topics. If they come up, just be honest and tell them you are not comfortable discussing this.
3. Meet in public places such as restaurants. Never be alone in your office or house.
4. Respect the privacy of the person you are mentoring. Don't share the information with others, unless it is for their safety.
5. Always set a positive example. Teaching integrity first means possessing it.

Chapter 6
A Message for the Youth

Parents, if you can talk your kids into reading this chapter, please do. Children must shoulder some of the responsibility in having a successful parent/child relationship as well.

Youth, this book was written primarily for parents. The *Factor of Eighteen* contains observations, suggestions, and ideas of how your parents can instill godly values in you by the time you are eighteen years old. However, you need to understand, you also have a role in cultivating a deeper, more meaningful relationship with your parents. Allow me to add some perspective.

When I was approximately thirteen years old, I worked for my dad at the miniature golf course he owned. Being the owner's son allotted me the luxury of the top end jobs; things like mopping the floor and scrubbing the toilets. Along with those duties, I also had to mow, pick up golf balls and refill the batting machines.

To the South of our driving range was a large field. On the other side of that field was another miniature golf course. They were our competitor. My dad and his partner spent a lot of time making improvements to our golf course. We needed to improve the business in order to increase our customer base. After a year or so, the miniature golf course was looking great. The number of customers had really increased over the last few months. We were in a position to compete with the more established miniature golf course on the other side of the field.

If my memory serves me correctly, I was fourteen at that time. It was a Friday night, which was one of our busiest nights of the week. My dad was curious to see how busy we were compared to our competitor. His partner was not there at the time; so he could not leave the clubhouse. Here's where the story got really exciting for me. My dad came to me and said, "I want you and David to take my car and drive over to the other golf course. Check and see how busy they are and then get back here as quickly as possible." David was my best friend. Before we go any farther with the story, in my dad's defense, there was a dirt road that connected the two golf courses. We never had to drive on any public roads to get there. So, my dad handed me the keys to his car. It was only a station wagon, not the most exciting ride, but for a fourteen year old kid, any car made for a fun ride. We drove down the gravel path heading to the dirt road around the corner that would take us to the other golf course. I looked in the rear view mirror and saw my dad watching us drive away from him. I continued to drive slowly and carefully. We finally turned the corner and were no longer in my dad's sight. I stopped the car and looked over at my best friend and said, "Are you thinking what I am thinking?" He said, "I think so, but what are you thinking?" I responded, "The last thing my dad told us to do was hurry back." David, then said, "That's exactly what he told us to do." Being the obedient son that I was, I certainly wanted to obey my father and hurry back. With a smile on my face, I placed the car in drive and put the pedal to the metal. With my eyes looking straight ahead and my hands at ten and two on the steering wheel, we proceeded down the dirt road. About five minutes later, or however long it takes a station wagon to go from zero to sixty, we hit a bump in the road. You would be amazed at how easily a station wagon can take flight when traveling at those speeds. All four wheels came off the ground and we were flying through the air. It seemed like time stopped for a moment. I remember looking over at David and seeing him staring at me. Fear filled his eyes and the smile was gone from his face. I'm sure I looked the same. The next thing I know, we are crashing to the ground with enough force that David hit his head on the dashboard and I hit mine on the steering wheel. I managed to get the car stopped. We then realized the horn is stuck and blaring quite loudly. Fortunately, when you are traveling at sixty miles per hour, it didn't take long to move far enough down the road to be out of my dad's hearing range. We opened the hood and managed to find the horn wire. We pulled it loose and shut off the horn. We were both okay and the horn was no longer sounding. We took a deep breath and realized everything was okay. We started to get back in the car to finish the short drive over to the other golf course before heading back to ours. My dad wouldn't know what happened and everything would be okay.

When David started to walk back to the passenger side of the car, he noticed the hubcap was missing on the front tire. It must have popped off on impact. We spent about fifteen minutes looking for it and never found it. We are now late getting back to the golf course. When we arrived, my dad was waiting for us and was not happy. He did his fatherly duty and gave me the "lecture" about being responsible and then sent us back to work. That evening when we were driving home from the golf course, my dad saw someone he knew in the next lane. He tried to honk the horn to get their attention. My dad appeared a little confused when the horn didn't work. Neither David nor I said anything to him, but we did smile at each other. My dad didn't question us about the horn not working at that time.

The best I can remember, I'm sure at least a month had passed since our driving fiasco, and no consequences had been given. David and I thought we were in the clear after that much time. However, the day of reckoning came and I remember it very vividly. My dad was outside working. He stuck his head in the door and asked me to come out and help him change the oil. As soon as I looked under the car, I knew I was in trouble. There was grass and dirt stuck all over the bottom of the car. Apparently, when we landed from our short flight, the front end of the car hit first and scooped up a large chunk of grass and dirt in the process. My dad noticed I saw the dirt and grass; so he asked me, "Do you know how this happened?" It was confession time. I owned up to the accident and exactly how it happened. I remember my dad being really cool about the whole situation. He used it as a teaching moment rather than a time to punish me. I didn't drive again anytime too soon. On the bright side, I did disprove the myth that station wagons can't fly.

I think my parents would tell you that I didn't cause them too much trouble. Like most every other kid, I made a few dumb decisions along the way, but I was pretty well-behaved. Obviously, my dad trusted me or he would not have given me the keys in the first place. I knew what I did was wrong, but chose to do it anyway because it seemed like fun at the time. However, now that I am a parent, and have my own child, my perspective has changed immensely. I now better understand my parent's actions. Some of the things my parents did, that I thought made no sense at all, now make perfect sense. Becoming a parent is a perspective changer for sure. Now that I am older, I look back and I am disappointed in myself for making the decision to drive my dad's car the way I did. I disappointed him because I didn't do what was expected of me. I took advantage of his trust. I'm sure there was a time frame after that in which I had to rebuild his trust in me. While my dad's response made perfect sense to me at that time, I know there were things my parents did that didn't make much sense to me.

Young people let me tell you that your parents love you more than you can imagine. Most parents would sacrifice anything and everything for you. I know there are exceptions for some kids, but this would apply to most of you. You will never totally understand your parents' perspective until you become parents yourselves. Until that time, you have to trust that your parents are doing what they believe is best for you. There are times your parents will make mistakes. They are imperfect people, but you must understand those mistakes are not intentional and are usually the result of an action that was meant to bless you. Your response in those moments will be a significant part of how your relationship is defined. You have a responsibility in developing and maintaining a healthy relationship with your parents as well.

You can only control you. Think about the things that create friction in your relationship with your parents. What's typically the bigger problem? Is it the apparent mistake your parents make, or your response to that mistake? Youth are telling me they want more freedom in their lives. Here's the perfect opportunity for you to use that freedom. You have the choice to determine how you will respond to your parents.

In Philippians 2:5, Paul tells us to have the attitude of Christ. In the context of this chapter, we see three main characteristics in Jesus' attitude. Those three things are humility, service, and obedience.

What might happen relationally with your parents if you applied those three characteristics to your relationship? If you displayed humility, were willing to serve your parents and obeyed them even when it's difficult, could you imagine how that would improve your relationships? Nearly all the teens I have spoken with strongly desire a better relationship with their parents. I know parents don't always respond in a favorable way to your desires and wants. I know you don't always understand why your parents do what they do. I know this can be frustrating. What is your typical response when this happens? Do you lose patience with your parents? Does anger creep into the picture? We, as parents, could certainly do things differently sometimes. However, now that I am a parent, I have a different perspective. Again, I now better understand why my parents did the things they did. There usually is a reason behind your parents' actions.

I would invite you on occasion to see things from their perspective. It might give you deeper insight into some of those frustrating moments. Parents and kids both have to change their perspective at times. At the end of the day, it's your relationship that matters. Parents still have to be parents. They get the final say.

I just want you to understand you have an important role in determining the depth of your relationship with your parents. Many kids rebel when parents discipline. That is the parents' God given role. Remember the attitude of Christ. Humility, service, and obedience will change the course of your relationship immensely. Even when your parents drop the ball, you are still accountable for your own response to them. See things from your parent's perspective, have the attitude of Christ, be patient when your parents make mistakes, and remember what they do will typically be prompted by their love for you. Take the initiative to deepen your relationship with your parents and see what happens. If not now, you will appreciate and respect your parents more as you grow older and wiser. Good luck and may God bless you as you support your parents in their God given roles.

Chapter 6 thought Questions: Parents and kids should discuss these together if possible. It might be difficult. Don't become angry at the answers or the person giving the answers. Be open and honest. Grow as a person from these responses.

1. What is the one thing that your parents do that creates the greatest strain on your relationship? With the understanding that your parents still have to be your parents, what are one or two things they could do to decrease this strain on your relationship?
2. Parents – what is the one thing your child does that creates the greatest strain on your relationship? From your perspective, how could they change this?
3. Plan something fun for all of you to do together. All parties must agree that it will be

enjoyable for all. If it has been a while since you have done something meaningful together, I would suggest keeping it short.

Chapter 7
Testimonies

The Factor of Eighteen is all about preparing our children to be the best person they can be. It's about instilling certain values in them before they leave home and head for college. It's about making sure they are developing integrity in their lives that will serve them well in their personal and professional lives.

I hope I have stressed the importance of this. I want you to hear from some young people; these are former students of mine. Whether one or both parents were not involved in their lives or both parents provided exactly what they needed, I want you to hear from them. It will help solidify the importance of our role as parents. The testimonies are unedited.

Testimony 1:

"With so many children coming from divorced parents you hear a lot of talk about girls with "daddy issues". This typically describes a girl who loves to party, disobeys any authority, changes with the wind to fit in, and will go to bed with just about anybody because she feels like it will fill that hole in her heart that her father left when her parents divorced.

Coming from a family with divorced parents I never quite understood the concept of trying to find love in other men. My father lived across the country and I never did have the urge to do such things. I got to see my dad once maybe twice a year, talked on the phone when holidays rolled around, and I still told him everything that was important to me. I felt like we had a great relationship considering the distance between us, and it wasn't until I was older that I realized that "daddy issues" went way deeper than going wild every weekend.

Although I did get to see my father every year, for every one time I did see him there were 5 broken promises of seeing him more. It seemed like every month he would promise to see me and every month my heart broke a little more. The amount of time spent talking to him lessened the older I got, and my heart broke because of that. Realizing that the constant rotation of my father's girlfriends far outweighed any time with me, broke my heart. I learned to expect the worst, and hope for the best when it came to the one man in my life who was supposed to love me like no other. Eventually, that flowed over into all of my relationships with any man.

When I was in high school there were two years that I hardly spoke with my father because of the arguing that came along with his new girlfriend. I knew deep down that my relationship with him was very important to me because throughout everything, I still loved him and valued his thoughts and opinions. So despite everything that happened with us, I sent him an invitation to my high school graduation and sent multiple e-mails to him asking him to let bygones be bygones and come watch me graduate. He finally promised me he would and had everything set, then a week before he was supposed to show up he backed out and never showed up. After that incident I realized how much him not being there for me affected me and I couldn't ignore it anymore.

Having boyfriends and always expecting them to fail you and let you down does only one thing...allows them to fail you and let you down. Because of the kind of relationship I had with my father, I don't trust any man to do well by me. I know deep down it isn't always the case, but I don't know any other way to think. I didn't have a positive father in my life to tell me how special and precious I am, to show me how a real man should treat a woman, how to trust somebody with your well-being. I believe those concepts are learned and without a father there to teach them to his little girl, it's pretty hard to understand it all.

Girls who grow up without a father don't like to think of themselves as having "daddy issues", but everybody handles pain differently. Whether it is partying every night to meet a new man, not trusting any man with your heart, or changing who you are constantly to try to be who others think you should be, those are all issues that stem from growing up without a father."

Testimony # 2:

"God has richly blessed me with the gift of my parents. I am currently 19 years old. The closer I come to the end of my "teen" years, the more I find myself thanking God for the parents that He has given me. I often stand amazed and in awe of God's goodness to me through the gift of my parents.

My parents recently celebrated their 27th wedding anniversary. As I searched through the card aisle in a nearby store, I finally found a card that I wanted to give to my parents. Inside the card I wrote the following note:

"Mom & Dad,

I cannot thank you enough for everything you've done for me and Spencer. Your willingness to be "open" and "real" has made a huge impact. Thank you for your stand for truth and godly example. I am absolutely blessed beyond measure to have you two as my parents. Not only do I consider you two my parents, but I count you as two of my closest friends and mentors.

Love you so much,
Hannah "

"I meant every word that I said in that card and I also believe that herein is where I find some of my parent's greatest influences in the parenting of both me and my brother. First, my parents have always been as open and candid as they could with us. Secondly, my parents have made and continue to make a stand for truth, some of which have cost them a great deal. And finally, my parents have set before me a godly example that is of infinite value.

Ever since I can remember, my parents have been straightforward and open with me and my brother.

Deuteronomy 6:4-7 says, "Hear, O Israel: The LORD our God, the LORD is one. You shall love the LORD your God with all your heart and with all your soul and with all your might. And these words that I command you today shall be on your heart. You shall teach them diligently to your children, and shall talk of them when you sit in your house, and when you walk by the way, and when you lie down, and when you rise." My parents have strived to do this very thing. Whether we are in the car or outside working together or talking on the phone, my parents have sought to use every aspect of life to teach us about Christ and God's Word. My parents have also been very open to us about their past. They often share the mistakes and sins that they committed in their past that we might learn from them and avoid doing the same thing. My parents have never once acted like they "have it all together" or tried to sweep past struggles and sins under the carpet. They have always been very straightforward and open with us when it comes to their mistakes in the past and the ones they make every day.

My entire life and to this day, I am the daughter of a preacher. My whole life, my father has been a pastor; sometimes full-time and others (like he is currently) bi-vocational. Having this privilege of being a daughter to a pastor, I have watched my father come into countless situations where he has had to stand for the truth of God's Word. I have also watched my mother come alongside my father and support him as he seeks to lead both the church and his family in the truth of God's Word. However, it has not only been in church that my parents have stood for truth. My parents have had to make stands for what is right in their places of employment, family, and dealings with other people. Almost all of these situations have not come without some cost. I have watched numerous people come and go from the church, I have heard the messages on the answering machine, I have read the letters, I have felt the stiffness in the air, and I have shed many tears. While some of these situations come very close to my heart, I can say as the writer of James did in James 1:2-4, "Count it all joy, my brothers, when you meet trials of various kinds, for you know that the testing of your faith produces steadfastness. And let steadfastness have its full effect, that you may be perfect and complete, lacking in nothing." Jesus tells us in Mathew 7:13-14 that the gate is narrow and the way is hard that leads to life and there are few who find it. So, if you would consider yourself a follower of Jesus Christ, you will come against some of these very battles when it comes to standing for truth. And be sure of this, that if you have children, they are watching to see just how precious this Jesus is to you. They are watching to see just how much you treasure Him. I can tell you from my own personal experience that it is not the stands that you make that are easy and cost you very little, but rather the stands that cost you greatly that will make an impact on your children. These are the times that your children will see the preciousness of Christ and be drawn closer to the Savior by God's help. If you face these types of trials in your life, and you display to your children a love for God and

His Word, then you will begin to set forth a godly example that will be of great value.

My parents have truly set a godly example for me and my brother. Their readiness to admit their mistakes, their willingness to be open, and their stand for truth have all culminated into their Christ-like example. There have been many things that my parents have recently discovered that they never did or instilled in us when we were young. However, my parents admit these things and by God's grace my brother and I see and understand what my parents are talking about and we seek to do these things with our own children. My parents have a generational vision and hope. They want their children to be more richly sanctified than they were and they desire even more for their grandchildren and great-grandchildren, Lord willing. This type of godly example extends beyond their lifetime. It will affect many generations to come. Now that I am older, I can begin to get a feel of just how valuable my parents are and have been to me. I have now moved into the phase of life where I can wholeheartedly say, just as I did in the card, that not only do I consider my parents my mother and father, but I also count them as two of my closest friends and mentors. My father reminds me quite often that I am now the age that he and my mother were when they got married. This is mind-boggling to me that I am now old enough to be married and have a family of my own. So, if the Lord so chooses to give me a husband and bless me with children one day, I know that the very example that my parents set before me will be displayed in the way I relate to my husband and children, Lord willing.

My parents will be the first to admit that they didn't do everything right and that there is a lot they wish they would have done differently. However, they are eternally grateful for the grace and mercy of God that has led us to where we are. By God's sovereign goodness and will, He will lead you to be parents that raise up mighty arrows for the kingdom of God (Psalm 127:4). I will never know many of the prayers and cries to God on me and my brother's behalf from my parents, but we recognize that without God's tender mercies and grace, we would be children of wrath just like the rest of mankind (Eph 2:3). Without God, these things are impossible, but with God all things are possible-even raising godly children (Mathew 19:26)."

Hannah Snow

Testimony 3:

"I have never doubted my parent's love for me. Although they are not perfect, I always knew I could talk to them about any situation or circumstance I was walking through. For as long as I can remember, my parents always dealt with the heart behind my actions. They would ask me questions to get me to think about the outcome of my decisions. They were extremely involved in my life without ever trying to control my life. They empowered me to make my own decisions. They would correct me when I was wrong; however,

they were never too prideful to come apologize to me when they had made a mistake. I remember so clearly the times my mother came to my room to apologize for something she said. It made me realize from a young age, the importance of a repentant and humble heart. Not only did it create a closer relationship between us as mother and daughter, it also gave me a deeper respect for her. My mom made me feel valued and known. She always made a point to ask me detailed questions about my life. Not only that, but she would pray with me when I was in the midst of a tough situation at school or with my friends. I also remember how my dad guarded and protected my emotions. He was so aware of the "unspoken," and knew how to draw it out of me while making me feel understood. I knew my dad fully trusted me, so in return, I desired to be completely honest and transparent with every situation I encountered. I never had any desire to rebel. There was nothing to rebel against. Sure, we had our moments of disagreements, but I always knew my parents loved me. They treated me like a child to be known, loved, and disciplined, not just a child to be corrected. They spent time with me and my siblings by asking one of us to go to the grocery store with them, or go on a bike ride together. They invested their lives into us and prayed daily for us. I am forever grateful for their example and unconditional love."

Joy Cales

Testimony 4:

"My mom and dad are two people that I have always looked at as my primary role models. I have always viewed my father as the protector and leader of our family. My mom has always been a determined, but incredibly compassionate and benevolent woman. They have sacrificed so much for me and still continue to do so although I am in my early 20s. I pray that I'll someday be able to teach my own children all the lessons they have taught me. I strive for my actions to match my words like they have always done.

My mom is my biggest role model in my life. She is always there for me when I want to talk. She'll tease me and joke around, but anytime I need to talk about something she's there for me. She'll listen to me ramble, give me encouragement, and give me reassurance through the Bible. I continuously respect her because she continues to amaze me in what she accomplishes. She recently obtained her Master's Degree from Liberty University in Theological Studies. I only hope to understand and know the Bible as well as I think she does. She is often encouraging me to find answers I have about the Bible for myself rather than just asking her.

She grew up in a very dysfunctional home and decided long ago that she did not want the same for her own family. I am blessed that my parents got saved before I was born because my life would have been very different. However, from day one I know my sister and I were prayed over and taught about our loving, merciful, and perfect God. My mom was determined and didn't let anyone ever tell her no. She was one of the first from her family to graduate with a college degree. My dad and she put forth a lot of effort every day to make sure we were always taken care of and felt loved. Even though my family was blessed financially, they never overly spoiled us to make sure we'd become responsible adults and realize that life isn't that easy and things are never just handed over to us.

My dad worked really hard in his twenties to get where he is today. He wanted to be able to provide for our family and that he did. It is because of his hard work that I have been so blessed to see the many things that I have and go to the incredible Christian school that I did.

He has always been a man of integrity. Sometimes I think his heart is too big for his own good. He often thinks of others before himself. Of course there were those awkward years of being a girl that I didn't want to talk to my dad about too much. However, he was patient with me and I know now that he is great at giving some amazing Godly advice I have tried to apply in my own life and will continue to do so. He is hilarious and always keeps our family laughing. I couldn't imagine my life without the rock and asset he is to my amazing and crazy family.

Through my psychology courses, I have learned that are several different parenting/ teaching styles. I quickly realized that my parents definitely raised me with an authoritative parenting style. They always gave me love and affection, but always disciplined me when I was in the wrong. This happened more times than I care to admit. Although I most certainly got yelled at from time to time, my parents tried hard not to lose their tempers (however I'm sure I made them want to innumerable times.) Instead they would ask me why I did what I did. They reasoned with me and explained why I was being disciplined.

My parents have always been very involved in my life. It is because of them (and of course God) that I am where I am in life. I can't even begin to count how many times my dad came home from a long day of work to talk to us about school or to play with us. He never complained about us asking him to play catch with us. Instead he would just grab his glove and go out and help us get better. This continued all the way up through my high school athletic career. My mom and dad were always there on the sidelines encouraging me. I could probably count on one hand the games that neither one of my parents came to. It didn't matter if it was t-ball, soccer, basketball, volleyball, or softball. They also came to every school concert, dance recital, piano recital, church play, and everything that we were involved in. My mom was always there. My dad came to pretty much all of them as well, even if he had to leave the office a few hours early or had to take off a weekend for a tournament. If he wasn't there, I knew he wanted to be, but couldn't be because of work. Seeing both of them there constantly gave me motivation to do better and to make them proud. I knew of their expectations of me and worked hard to meet them. It is a natural part of my personality to do so. I hate people being upset at me or disappointing anyone. Therefore, it was obvious for me to please them and make my parents want to brag about me. I say all of this, however, there were many games that I walked away from knowing that I could have done a lot better and felt rather discouraged. My mom and dad gave me some pointers to improve for the next game, but also always made sure I didn't blame myself. They always reminded me that even the pros have off games and that there was nothing I could do about it because it was in the past. So, I may as well cheer up and work hard to do better the next time around. (Sometimes ice cream really helped here as well.)

My parents took us to church all the time and urged us to read the Bible ourselves for answers. They never shoved religion in my face, but rather gently showed me what was right and wrong according to God's Word. They allowed me to be confident in who I was and who I was in Christ. They never tried to make me be different than who I was. They always encouraged me to be me and to be unique. One of my favorite scripture passages in Psalm 139. I have read this plenty of times. One would think I should have it memorized by now. At any rate, my parents often reminded me of the truth of this chapter as well as the fact that I was made in the image of Christ. I do still have to continue reminding myself of these truths even today. They continue to teach me what it means to be a true, devoted Christ follower. There is no talking the talk without walking the walk in my family. What you get is what see. Some people may not agree with us, but looking at family that is not walking with the Lord, I believe God has his hand on my parents and have guided them along the way. My family may be silly, loud, sometimes annoying, but I wouldn't trade any of them for the world. I am so blessed for my three siblings to be three of my very best friends, especially my twin sister. I cannot imagine what I would do without that remarkable girl in my life. Every time I talk to either one of my parents on the phone, I always end the phone call with, "I love you." I never want them to forget that I truly mean that and that I'm so thankful of the sacrifices they have made for me. I only esteem and respect them more as I get older. I'm sure one day when I'm married and have kids of my own; my eyes will be opened to whole new world of appreciation for them. My mom and dad tell me just about every time I go home now that they love me and that they're proud of me. That means the world to me. Every time."

~Amanda Sauer

Testimony 5:

When I think about my parent's impact on my life, 3 things immediately jump to my mind: love, discipline, and guidance.

The biggest thing I remember is the love they have always given me and continue to give although I am evolving into an adult now. It was never a selfish love like someone who does things for you only to be your friend for the day. Instead, my parents sacrificed for me and my siblings. I am pretty sure my parents would have liked to enjoy their 25th wedding anniversary alone on a cruise instead of bringing their 4 teenagers along, but they knew it would be an unforgettable experience for us. And as I look back on the years, all the time and money they spent so that we could go to a school with the Lord in the heart of it or going to hundreds of sports games and musical events over the years was very much appreciated. I will not forget my mom going on elementary field trips with my class or my parents allowing me to have 10 preteen, hyper girls over for my birthday, which I am sure caused them to go to bed with a headache. I could go on and on of times I know my parents gave of themselves so their children could enjoy the beautiful gift of life. I know I took for granted many of the things my parents did for me, but I still enjoyed every time they supported me in something I wanted to and felt that I could make them proud. They often made a point of how important family should be to us and showed that through their actions. It was through their repetitive actions that I could trust them and believe each time they said to me, "I love you." I am not trying to just make this just "sound good," but truly know the love my parents have for me. I know I did not tell them thank you enough, because although I did not say something, their sacrifices did not go unnoticed.

Also, I grew up in a house unafraid of discipline. I think they made it a priority to not give in to their adorable children and I have seen old pictures: it must have been hard! I never remember being given that toy I was eyeing in Wal-Mart I saw on TV because I screamed or cried about it. Of course, I do not recall every day of my life when I was three, but my mom has since told me she did not have to worry about how I would act in the store. I am not saying I was perfect because every child is going to pout on occasion. It also could have been easier because my sister and I were some of the shyest girls I have ever seen. But, I also know that two 6 yr olds, a 4 yr old, and 2 yr old could not have been an easy task to manage every day. Very importantly, my parents followed through with their words. That was probably key in my growing up because I feel that too many parents today do not follow through with all the warnings they give their children and thus, soon do not believe when their parents say they will discipline them. Until I moved out, if I did something I was warned or knew not to do, I was punished in some way. I feel this mold me in giving respect and obedience to not only my parents, but to other adults. Because my parents enforced the rules at home, whether I liked them or not, it taught me that importance and protection of rules. I grew up with enforced rules, so being honest, I typically did not try to break them, so in turn, I did not get into any serious trouble growing up.

No matter how I was disciplined, they would often explain or have me say why I was punished.

I was taught that even "the Lord disciplines those he loves." As I look back on how my parents raised me, I do not think parents took lightly the verse Proverbs 22:6. They believed in the power of God's Word and did their best to train us up in the way of the Lord. What I think could be most useful to molding my life now has been their guidance. My mother and father did not just tell us what was best or what we should do, but showed us in their daily lives. They might not know how much I still look at their lives and hope I can model half of what they have done for others and for the Lord. I do know it is only because of their continual seeking and personal time with God they have been a good example on their children. Because they guided me at a young age to have my own time with God, like doing short Bible studies at the breakfast table with my dad, I am still challenged in my own spiritual life every day to do so. Another example is their modeling the heart of a servant.

I am amazed how much my dad is willing to help and serve others or my mom willing to let anybody stay at our house for a week or for the whole summer. As I saw that growing up, I am now realizing it is my responsibility as a Christian to have that constant servant attitude that Jesus Christ had. It is not very easy, but it is not supposed to be. Otherwise, there would not be a blessing for those who do so with a righteous heart.

Another great example of their guidance is how my parents treated each other. They have had some good and bad times just like any other marriage, but they have portrayed a Godly marriage, full of love, trust, and definitely a lot of laughter. Laughter has been a constant thing in my parent's household which is one thing I often miss. As I am a young adult now, I can prepare myself and pursue that kind of marriage for my future and am able to see what a Godly marriage looks like in order for me to model some day. I think this is something that has really been brought to my attention and noticed more because of the season of life I am in. I have seen how a husband is to be the leader of a family, protect his children to love his wife as Christ loves us, and most importantly to keep God as a priority. This is what I am able to expect in my future husband. Also, as I have seen how nurturing my mom was to us and how she not only served my dad but submitted to him as his wife, I see how I should prepare myself for that kind of commitment to be a Godly wife. Of course my parents were not perfect and I saw them struggle sometimes, but I am confident enough to say that I want my future marriage to model theirs. I have been very blessed to have live under a home that encouraged me and guided me in my own personal relationship with God. Simply put, it was because I saw my parents strive to have God in the center of our home, not by force, but through His love that shown through them that cause me to continually seek Him now in my own life."

Ashley Sauer

Fathers, we especially need to step up to the plate and be more active in the lives of our children. We can have a huge impact on our sons and daughters. You read the statistics and know that is true. You also read a testimony of one young lady who did not have her father involved in her life. It is a sad situation and that broken relationship still impacts her today.

I admire and respect all the single parents. Your job is so difficult. My wife and I only have one child. Even though we help each other, it can still be exhausting at times. I don't know how you do it by yourselves. You have my deepest admiration, but you will have to work extra hard on the factor of eighteen.

Find a mentor for your children. Statistics are showing tremendous hope, especially for our young men, who have a positive male role model in their life. There really is hope, but you must be very proactive with this approach.

Remember, this is all about keeping the end in mind. What values are you trying to instill in them before they turn eighteen? Who can help you do this the best? Get them on board.

As we clearly see from statistics, first-hand experience, and observing other families, we must fight to keep the family intact. Generally speaking it gives our children the best fighting chance. Sometimes that requires sacrifice in a marriage in order to allow our children to prosper.

In this chapter you have read testimonies of people I know personally. They clearly demonstrate how important it is for parents to be involved in their lives; it is absolutely essential. Our kids need us more than ever. Our culture is bombarding them with drugs, pornography, anti-religious propaganda, and a host of other destructive philosophies. How we love and protect our children will be crucial in the outcome of this war being waged against our youth today.

Chapter 7 thought questions:

1. Name one to three possible mentors for your children.
2. Why would each of these people be a wise choice?
3. In what areas do your children most need mentoring to help them reach those desired character traits by the time they are 18?
4. Are you in a position to mentor anyone? If so, who might that be and how could you help?

Conclusion

The future has arrived. Your child is eighteen. You are helping him/her load the car. They are about to drive away for college. You try to start a conversation, but the lump in your throat won't let you. The emotions of the moment are too powerful. You stop loading the car and watch your child for a moment. You find out what was mentioned earlier in this book is true – your mind is flooded with his childhood memories.

In that moment, what do you see as the end product? What qualities does your child possess? Is he where you want him to be? Would you go back and change anything in your parenting style? Would you hug him more? Would you be more patient? Would you have worked a few less hours? Does television seem a little less important in that moment? Would you have worked harder at instilling values that would carry him through the college years?

Picture those thoughts as you are reaching out and embracing your child one more time before they drive several hours away to college. What is really important to you in that moment?

If your child is not that old yet, get very busy doing those things that matter the most. Be involved, be supportive, teach values, mentor or find mentors, pray with your child, live with integrity. Do all those things that will influence the factor of eighteen. That way, when they are eighteen, you can embrace them one more time and know you were not perfect, but you did all you could do. In that moment you will realize all the sacrifices you made were well worth it. Your child understands that he/she is loved. You have instilled proper values and they have embraced those values. As a parent you have been instrumental in the factor of eighteen. Has it been worth it? I can only imagine looking my son in his eyes during that goodbye hug and saying to myself, it was absolutely worth it. Wise investing typically produces great dividends. What a blessing and reward it will be to see your sons and daughters walking the path that leads to success.

If you already have a great relationship with your children, keep doing what you have been doing. Make adjustments when necessary, but stay involved. If you need to start over, now is the time. Make it a priority to be a key influence in your children's lives and become the Factor of Eighteen.